12 UNIVERSAL
SKILLS

**HEADWAY
SKILLS**

12 UNIVERSAL SKILLS

THE BEGINNER'S GUIDE
TO A SUCCESSFUL
WORK LIFE

**Peter Scheele
& Nina Bech-Andersen**

**HEADWAY
SKILLS**

HEADWAY SKILLS

Estepona, Malaga, Spain
Headwayskills.com

Editing: Shayla Raquel
Cover Design: Colibrian

ISBN: 978-84-09-43287-5 (paperback), 978-84-09-43612-5 (hardback), 978-84-09-43613-2 (epub), 978-84-09-43615-6 (audiobook)

CONTENTS

PREFACE

Our motivation for writing this book is to break the chain of the many who start their careers full of excitement, high expectations, and fresh ideas . . . but end up making the same mistakes as those before them, learning through trial and error. We believe it's time to disrupt this pattern. There's no reason why anyone should start their career without the information and tools that can help them navigate their new environment and build the foundation for a happy and successful work life.

So if you're about to start your career, or are in the first five years of your career, this book is for you. It's packed with the skills you need to not only survive but to thrive and succeed.

As experienced managers, we've seen many people (at all levels) struggle, including ourselves in our early years. But it doesn't have to be so. That's why we've created the 12 universal skills, including many rules and practices that are usually untaught and unwritten, to ease the transition.

With this knowledge, you can accelerate your learning curve when you start your career and avoid a ton of unnecessary mistakes. What's more, you'll better understand the skills and strengths you already possess so you can make the most of them and perform more effectively in your job.

This book specifically focuses on those with little or no work experience. That's different from most books in this genre, which take for granted that they speak to an experienced audience, typically at the management level. Additionally, we've tried to cover all the main skills in one place. That's also different from other books, which typically go in-depth with only one topic. Communication. Teamwork. Resilience. Influence. And so on. One book for each skill. Here we have identified the 12 most important skills and dedicated a complete chapter to each. Consequently, this book is quite condensed; there's no fluff here! Instead, it's a how-to book filled with actionable tips and techniques in plain language.

So, how did we make this book?

Besides our careers, we've always been ardent students of many topics related to business and organizational life: strategy, organizational theory, psychology, communication, leadership, and more. This interest gave us the foundation (and a huge library of relevant literature). Writing this book was only a natural next step, driven by what we experienced in our jobs, where we routinely worked with many at the start of their work life. We clearly saw the need for some kind of guide that could ease and advance the transition from the school system to professional career.

Starting the project, we spent the first year doing research, including reading yet another batch of relevant books to test and expand our own knowledge. We still had much to learn (actually, we're always learning!). Then we shared our idea bank with a diverse group of experienced people that we admire for their great interpersonal skills, success, and balanced lives. We carried out interviews with soon-to-be graduates before they started their first professional job to hear what their expectations and fears were. Others we interviewed after the start of their careers to understand how they actually experienced their transition to work life.

Next was the writing phase. To ensure we captured different perspectives and kept the content practical, we formed a small reference group of three individuals with exceptional people skills and strong personal integrity. Now we had the perfect team to discuss everything with, and get honest feedback from. When the full book draft was ready, we (again) had it challenged by a new group of business experts and leaders across the globe. Finally, we asked young people at the start of their careers to read it—and found yet a new round of needed revisions. Only then were we satisfied that we had done everything we could to get it right!

As this story indicates, this book is a practitioner's guide, not an academic work. Of course, research has inspired some of the content (see the notes for some outstanding resources), but everything here is hands-on, practical advice.

At a late stage in the project, we realized that the 12 universal skills were also highly relevant for job searchers. So we decided to add an appendix about job search, tying it to the 12 universal skills. That way, this book also serves as an in-depth job search guide—with a special focus on those who are early in their careers or looking for their first job or an internship. But the appendix is equally relevant for those looking for an internal move in their current organization, as most of the practices are the same.

On our website, headwayskills.com, you'll find a collection of resources (tools and templates) to assist your reflection and learning. We encourage you to go to the website and download whatever you find useful. The content is organized by skill, and we're sure you'll find additional value. It's all free.

Finally, if you find this book helpful, please leave a brief review on Amazon, Goodreads, or any other site you prefer.

Good luck with using it all and creating a successful work life.

Peter Scheele
Nina Bech-Andersen

INTRODUCTION

Every year, millions of new graduates from all kinds and levels of education enter the global workforce. And for many, the transition from the school system to work life isn't straightforward—because there are nontechnical skills that are really important in the workplace they haven't learned. These skills are often called "soft skills" or "employability skills." Learning them is a huge opportunity for everyone.

Soft skills are, for example, interpersonal skills like communication and teamwork, interacting with your manager, and professional etiquette. They're also self-regulatory skills that help you gain confidence and manage yourself in all kinds of situations. Many people are only half-conscious about their soft skills; these skills are often *unspoken* rules and practices, which is why people often learn them in a trial-and-error way, while some never quite get it right.

"Hard skills," on the other hand, are the factual skills you get from the school system—like how to structure a computer program, how to administer an injection, how to make a marketing plan, or how to build a staircase.

As an example, let's imagine you're working in a bank and you're dealing with an angry and unreasonable customer. In that situation, your soft skills determine how you interact with the customer and how you handle the situation emotionally. But your hard skills are your knowledge of what types of loans you can offer the customer, under what conditions.

Despite soft skills being essential in the workplace, teaching them isn't necessarily defined as anyone's responsibility. Some schools and universities, as well as some large organizations, make a good effort. But others don't have much to offer—if anything at all.

We aim to fill this gap with the 12 universal skills. We try to give you a shortcut to what usually takes years of experience to understand, learn, and leverage. Of course, you've already picked up some (hopefully excellent) soft skills from parents and siblings, friends, school, previous work experiences, volunteer activities, and so on, and they are your *foundation*. Now, when reading this book, you can better understand what valuable skills you already have and start adding to them.

How Critical Are Soft Skills?

Teams of people with excellent soft skills can make the most spectacular results. Oppositely, when people or teams have significant gaps, things go wrong. Sometimes terribly wrong. Even at the executive level of organizations, relationship difficulties may be central in creating problems that often have far-reaching and negative consequences.

Ask any experienced leader, and you'll get the answer that soft skills are indeed very important. Those who struggle with soft skills often have difficulties working with others. And at work, you are *always* working with others; being successful is much more than "doing my job" and reaching your targets. To be sure, hard skills obviously *also* matter a lot, and they often land you your first job. But in the interview process, recruiters will usually scan equally as much for soft skills, looking for communication, teamwork, and influencing skills—or just plain old-fashioned good behaviors and etiquette. That's how important these skills are.

A great thing about soft skills is that they are highly transferable between jobs; good people skills and self-management skills are *always* useful, regardless of which industry you're in, which organization you work for, or which role you're in. And they never become obsolete. That's why we call this book *12 Universal Skills*: because the skills are universally useful and applicable.

As you progress through your career, hard skills often recede more into the background, and soft skills weigh *even* more. In the same way, lack of soft skills may hold you back from achieving what you want. So take this book seriously:

learning these skills may be one of the best investments you will ever make. These skills are essential not only for your career but for your work life in general. They are instrumental to your well-being and satisfaction at work and to keeping a healthy work-life balance.

How Do I Learn Soft Skills?

First, let's establish that soft skills are *learnable*; they are not reserved for especially talented or privileged people. Soft skills are for everybody, regardless of background and previous experience. And where you have gaps, you can regard them as something you just haven't learned *yet*. Your gaps are changeable.

Put simply, the way to learn the skills is through *practice*—like any other skill. The difference with soft skills is that the learnings are in the personal and interpersonal space and thus require behavior changes. For instance, how to constructively tackle conflicts. But they do not require modifications of personality or values. You can still be *you*.

Some skills you'll have to practice repeatedly to make them stick. And you'll probably have to go back to this book and reread specific sections. Which skills *you* find easy—or difficult—is an individual thing, as some skills will come naturally to you, while others will challenge you and require you to move beyond your comfort zone. Some skills will be quick to learn, while others will take much longer.

But we promise you it'll be worth it.

Ultimately, to create a successful work life, you want to be at least moderately proficient in most of the skills. Nobody is perfect in all of them, but try to ensure you don't have *big* gaps. And try to have some areas where you stand out and shine.

The Skills Required at Work

Compared with the school setting, the skills you need to succeed at work may differ significantly. Acceptable, good, or even great habits in the school system may not fit at work. Or may even work against you. Additionally, completely *new* skills may be required.

Let's walk through some of the differences between work life and life as a student:

- At work, people are evaluated not only for their hard skills but also for their soft skills. And the soft skills often weigh as much as the hard skills; people with great professional behaviors are highly valued (and rewarded) by organizations. That differs from schools, where students are usually only evaluated for their academic performance, or their hard skills. No grades are given for soft skills. That means, for example, that the bullying and exclusive behaviors that are frequently found in schools will, generally, have more severe negative consequences in the workplace.

- In your work life, you can follow your interests and natural strengths. You can create a career path that feels right for *you*. And you can change direction if you discover a new strength or interest. That's a welcome change for the many who found the structure of the school system stifling and felt forced to study topics they had little or no interest in. At the same time, this freedom requires self-awareness and sound judgment to make the best choices.

- Communication is a substantial part of most jobs; in some, it's the biggest part. And that differs from life as a student, where you may have days or weeks without much need to communicate with anyone. Also, the communication channels often differ, and there's more at stake when communication goes wrong.

- At work, you are working *with* others, not against them. You are not in competition with your colleagues; quite the opposite, you are paid to be effective *together*. The point of evaluation is the *team's* performance—more than it is any individual's performance. That differs from the school system, which may sometimes seem like a competition for good grades and the attention of your teachers. And that feeling of being in a competition can lead to habits that are unproductive at work. For example, holding back on opinions or possible "stupid" questions. Or hiding or trying to fix mistakes alone. Or keeping your best stuff for yourself and not sharing it. Habits like these actually need to be *reversed* in the workplace.

- You don't have a manager in the school system; you are, more or less, your own manager. Authorities like teachers and administrators are important, but they are not your *manager*. That is, of course, different in organizations, where it's your manager's job to ensure that you're effective and happy in your job. But you also need to do *your part* in making it a productive relationship—for many, that's a new skill they need to learn.

- In the same way as you're your own manager in the school system, you're also your own timekeeper: you decide how much to work and how deep or shallow you go with each task. For instance, you can choose to spend hours refining things to perfection. Or you can do the bare minimum and instead spend your time with friends; it may have no influence on your academic performance. That changes at work because you have to optimize your time for the needs of your job and not so much for yourself. Which means lower intellectual freedom, as you don't necessarily get to decide how to spend your time.

- Finally, you're a pretty homogeneous group in the school system. You are all more or less the same age. You are all students. And often, you are from similar backgrounds and cultures. That's some contrast to most workplaces where you'll likely work with a very diverse crowd of people. Consequently, you'll need to adapt to a much more diverse environment where you work with people from many age groups, professions, countries, cultures, backgrounds, etc.

The 12 Universal Skills

These many differences between work life and life as a student call for a different skill set. And the idea of this book is to function as a guide to the most important skills. The skills are broad and range from self-regulatory skills (like building confidence), over behavioral skills (like interacting with your manager), to proactive behaviors (like networking). It might sound like a lot, but truth be told, that's what it takes to ensure a successful work life.

SKILL 1

BUILDING SELF-AWARENESS

- Find and focus on your natural strengths.

- Know your biases and iceberg beliefs.

- Feedback is your fuel. Remember to refuel often.

To develop yourself in your job, you need to continually build and improve your self-awareness. In a way, self-awareness is the most important skill: it's the fundamental building block for all the other skills.

And there's a *big* upside to gaining more self-awareness: you have natural strengths you're probably not aware of or don't use much that can be brought to your attention with improved self-awareness. That's your hidden potential. And when you know this potential, new possibilities open up, such as natural strengths that weren't that relevant for academic accomplishment but can be instrumental in your work life—for example, natural strengths within influencing and relationship building.

Likewise, there's an upside to knowing what might be holding you back: you can do something about it.

Building self-awareness requires an open mind. It means being willing to accept that other people have a right to have a different view. And, more challenging, it means actively *seeking* others' views to test and possibly disconfirm your own views.

Natural Strengths

Your natural strengths and weaknesses are the traits and characteristics that make you *you*. They are your unique qualities that don't change (much) over your lifetime. For example, some people are naturally talented at making and following routines and structure; others at creating new ideas and finding alternative ways (but not necessarily at following routines). Some people are naturally empathetic and easily sense other people's feelings; others have their natural strengths in thinking and analyzing (but not necessarily in sensing other people's feelings). And some people are at their best with open-ended, ambiguous, and risky work; others perform best with well-defined work (and don't like risky and open-ended work).

This book emphasizes *strengths* rather than weaknesses. Understanding your natural strengths enables you to focus on what you do best. You don't have to be good at everything. That's a defensive strategy (and it's impossible). It's much more productive to build on your natural strengths.

Identifying your natural strengths probably sounds easy. If anyone knows what they are, that should be you, right? You know yourself . . . or do you? In fact, identifying one's natural strengths *can* be difficult because it's easy to get confused.

First, you may be *good* at something without *enjoying* it. This often concerns a skill that you've acquired and do well but would still prefer *not* to do. For example, if it's a mandatory part of your job to write some formal documents, you may have acquired the skills to do what is required. You may even get compliments for your writing style. But that says nothing about whether or not you *like* writing them. Maybe, in reality, you dread those documents, procrastinate, and feel unmotivated when you write them. So it's entirely possible to be good at something that's *not* a natural strength.

Second, you may *not have encountered* some of your natural strengths *yet*. For example, let's assume that hosting meetings is a strength you just haven't discovered yet. You may never have done this in a formal way and, in the beginning, will make mistakes, but you'll quickly pick it up. You'll notice that you enjoy the process of planning meetings and preparing with the different participants, and you'll feel energized when hosting them. You'll feel that it somehow comes naturally to you. In this case, you'll *discover* a natural strength. But if someone had asked you before, you wouldn't have known that you had this natural strength.

Third, you may find some things so *easy* that you don't consider them strengths; you just assume that everybody else *also* finds them easy. But they may not. For example, let's say you've just finished working on something when you receive an email from a colleague saying that it needs "several improvements." If interpersonal communication is a natural strength, you would just find that person—or make a call—and ask what needs to be improved. Simple! That reaction would be natural and obvious for you; you wouldn't even consider that there could be other ways to react. But there *are* different reactions; some people avoid personal communication and answer by email instead—or start looking for errors on their own instead of asking.

With these possible confusions in mind, the best way of identifying your natural strengths is by using some self-evaluation questions. They come in three categories: the way you work, how it makes you feel, and your results.

About the *way you work*: Which activities . . .

- come naturally and easily to you?
- are you more creative and productive in?
- do you try over and over again without giving up?
- do you learn quickly?
- make you get so absorbed that you lose track of time?

About how it makes you *feel*: Which activities do you . . .

- look forward to?
- enjoy doing?
- feel strong when doing; feel are "the real *me*"?
- get energized from, even if you work for a long time?
- feel satisfied and proud about when finished?

About your *results*: Which activities do you . . .

- do better than other people?
- get praised for; think others see *you* as being good at?

In addition to the above questions, you can also use tests to identify your natural strengths. There are a lot to choose from, both strengths tests and personality tests, but take more than one test so you can gain perspective. Some suggestions can be found at headwayskills.com/resources. With the results in hand, take them with a grain of salt. This is no exact science, but on the other hand, these results *do* give you direction and clues if you answer the questions honestly. If you think that some of the results are off, that's fine, but watch out for self-denial. If there is *some* truth in the results (and you deep down know that), it's better to start accepting who you are. That's the whole point of self-awareness. It's also good to discuss your test results with a few friends, family members, or colleagues who know you well. They can usually help you see which parts of the results fit you and which don't.

Biases

We all feel that we are objective and see the world correctly. This is deeply rooted in human behavior: we think *our* beliefs and values are special and right. Unfortunately, some of our beliefs and values may have taken shape as unhelpful *biases*. And we may not even be aware of them because they're a product of our upbringing and culture. They are deeply integrated into who we are.

But biases create problems at work. First, discrimination resulting from biases is unjust and is a loss for the organization. Second, biases can get you into conflicts with people you discriminate against and those who see it (even if you do it unconsciously and without ill intentions). So it's appropriate to do some self-evaluation to identify which biases you may have. For instance, consider if you think that one group is better than another—if you think so, then you likely have a bias.

Some classical biases that create problems are stereotypical and discriminatory biases for men versus women, immigrants versus residents, one country versus another, and one ethnic group versus another. Or biases against political or religious affiliation, education, age, height, weight, attractiveness, sexual orientation, language, dialect, city, and even which part of the city people are from. Social class is also a strong bias. If you're from the working class, you may have been brought up with a suspicion of people occupying management positions. And vice versa, if you come from a prosperous background, you may have been brought up with prejudice against people with less fortunate backgrounds. People's jobs also easily lead to biases. When people hear about other people's jobs, they often immediately—and unconsciously—categorize them: "Oh, you're from IT" or "Oh, you work in the warehouse."

The ability to work with a wide variety of people is a must. Everyone has biases to some degree, so take an honest look in the mirror and try to identify your own. For example, looking for those mentioned here. Then, challenge yourself to treat everyone impartially and with an open mind. And try to catch yourself thinking or behaving with bias. For example, when you find that you jump to conclusions regarding someone else's skills or behaviors.

Iceberg Beliefs

As with biases, your deep rules and beliefs about how the world "should" operate are a product of your upbringing and culture. They are beliefs formed in childhood long ago, and you probably don't know or remember anything about where they came from. Psychologists call these beliefs "iceberg beliefs" because they work unconsciously, existing like icebergs under the water where you don't see them. And you may not even think of them as beliefs because they are so integrated into your identity. They function like *facts* that you take for granted and probably never question.

Many iceberg beliefs are positive and realistic, for example:

- It's important to be honest.
- It's important to allow people to tell *their* version of a story.
- I don't give up when something becomes difficult.
- Most people like me.

However, some iceberg beliefs are negative and unrealistic. They stem from childhood experiences and still control parts of your thoughts and behaviors. They are positive when people have them at a *normal* degree—but problematic when exaggerated. They are very common, and most people will recognize a bit of these beliefs in themselves.

Psychologists have grouped iceberg beliefs into three types.

The first type is achievement-oriented. This is about setting high standards for oneself and aiming for success, which is fine at normal levels. However, people with an *exaggerated* need for achievement often have unrealistically high standards and expectations of themselves and others. They may feel anxious about their own performance and be highly critical of other people's contributions, leading to conflicts. Many are perfectionists, spending too much time on things and focusing too much on mistakes and imperfections. Here are some examples of typical exaggerated achievement beliefs:

- A person is only valued by achievement, by "success."
- Failure is a sign of weakness.
- I must not be seen as incompetent.
- I must never give up.
- It has to be perfect.

The second type is acceptance-oriented. This is about wanting others' acceptance—again, absolutely fine at normal levels. However, people with an *exaggerated* need for acceptance are more likely to overreact to interpersonal conflicts. Or assume that other people don't like them (even when it's unfounded). For example, if someone does not greet them or is silent. They may also try too hard to please others or may be attention-seeking. Or they may try too hard to gain praise or boast about accomplishments. To avoid conflict or rejection in situations involving differing opinions, they may say things they don't believe or (oppositely) *not* say the things they *do* believe. Here are some examples of typical exaggerated acceptance beliefs:

- I must make sure that people think the best of me.
- I must make sure that other people are happy.
- I must avoid conflict no matter what.
- I must avoid embarrassment.
- It's wrong to hurt other people's feelings.

The third type is being control-oriented. This is about wanting to be in charge and having control—absolutely fine at normal levels. However, people with an *exaggerated* need for control are uncomfortable when things are out of *their* control—and their "fix" is to *take* control. Consequently, other people may see them as "control freaks." Or, when things turn out *un*successfully, they blame themselves for not having taken control. To avoid showing vulnerability, a control-oriented person may avoid asking questions, asking for help, or asking for feedback. Here are some examples of typical exaggerated control beliefs:

- I must always be seen as strong.
- I must not show my feelings.
- I have to do it myself if I want it to be right.
- Asking for help is a sign of weakness.
- Only cowards bend under pressure.

Iceberg beliefs can work against you in your career. But luckily, they can be controlled and changed. So take a moment and look inward. Do you (to some extent) have any of the exaggerated iceberg beliefs? Don't worry if you think you do because the first remedy is to actually *acknowledge* them. Then they are not "icebergs" anymore; by just being aware of them, you are already on your way to adopting more balanced views. What's more, many of the skills in this book are very useful for controlling and reducing negative iceberg beliefs.

For example, goal setting, confidence building, professional behaviors, team behaviors, communication, and personal effectiveness. So, read on.

Feedback

So far, this chapter has been about *self*-evaluation. But self-evaluation can only take you to the limits of your own knowledge and experience. You need external input—feedback from others—to develop. Feedback *fuels* your development. That goes for everybody, including experts and managers and people with twenty-five years of experience; they still need to develop.

Feedback can come from just about everyone, not just from your closest colleagues or your manager. You can potentially get input from everybody you have interactions with. Feedback can be anything from small daily interactions where people help or correct you, to formal performance reviews. The trick is to get the most out of it all.

Importantly, feedback comes in two kinds:

1. *Developmental* feedback, which is when the feedback giver is trying to help you grow and develop. You'll see this in the form of advice and corrections so you can learn and improve. It's part of your daily work when people help you or correct you, and it can be about anything: from practical details about your work, to behaviors and other soft skills.

2. *Evaluative* feedback, which is when the feedback giver is grading or evaluating you compared with others or with some standard. It tells you how you're doing or how you measure up against expectations. For example, the grades used in the educational system and evaluations by managers, such as "You're doing well" or "You need to improve." Or feedback from colleagues, such as "Good job" or "It's not up to our standard."

Both kinds of feedback are needed, but many people think of feedback mainly as *evaluation*. They associate "feedback" with something potentially upsetting, especially if they think of negative evaluation or criticism. They hear or *feel* criticism even when it really *is* advice. And that's a pity because if you perceive feedback as *both* developmental and evaluative, it's a crucial source of helpful information. Used the right way, it's very constructive. You get advice on things you didn't know so you can work on them and get better. You get appreciation for what you do right so you can continue to build yourself in that direction. And you get information about what you should improve or stop doing.

Of course, feedback is the opinion of the person giving you the feedback. Their feedback may tell as much about *them* as about you. For example, if you have a busy desk with piles of papers and other stuff floating around, one person may think you have a lot to do and that you're very productive; whereas, another person may think you are too lazy to tidy up. Accordingly, they will give you very different feedback. But that difference would reflect on them, not you. And that's a fundamental principle of feedback: it is just another person's opinion, perception, or preferred way of doing things. It is not necessarily correct, even if they firmly hold their point of view. Think of their feedback as *their view* instead of something you should challenge. They have a right to their view just as you have a right *not* to share that view.

Consequently, when people give you feedback expressed as "*You* are . . . lazy/productive/whatever," you should translate it to "*He/she thinks* I am lazy/productive/whatever." What's important is to acknowledge that they *do* have this view, which should be respected. Nevertheless, if *more* people share the same view, it's no longer just one person's opinion. And then it's probably the kind of feedback you should seriously think about.

How we take feedback is very individual. Some people are relatively robust and comfortable even with negative feedback. Others tend to take all kinds of feedback to heart and easily get nervous or offended. If you're uncomfortable with feedback, here's some good news: everybody—including those who try to avoid feedback—can improve their skills. The rest of this chapter explains two sets of feedback skills: how to receive it and how to ask for it.

How to Receive Feedback

Feedback can be as informal and straightforward as getting a piece of advice or a quick correction or having a colleague review a sample of your work—or anything beyond that to formal feedback meetings with your manager. When you receive feedback, your goal should be to extract as much useful information out of it as possible. To do that, use the technique described below.

Step One: Understand the Feedback

First—and most importantly—focus on *understanding* the feedback: what exactly is meant by it? What is the context: *where, when*, and *how* did the feedback giver observe or hear *what*? When you listen, listen to understand, not to argue. You can ask as many questions as you like, but the purpose of the questions should be to *clarify*. For example, say, "Tell me more, as I want to understand." If you sense that you react emotionally, try to separate your emotions from the feedback; try to see the feedback as just *information* coming from this person.

If the feedback is vague or imprecise, try to find out what *specifically* the feedback is. You want something concrete you can actually work on or implement. For example, if someone said, "You have to be more active in meetings," that could mean many things. Maybe they mean that you should pay more attention and not get distracted by your phone or laptop. Or maybe they mean you should offer more of your ideas and knowledge and not hold back or be shy. Perhaps they want you to ask more questions or take part in discussions. The meaning may be clear for the person who gives the feedback, but not for you. And then, what should you do differently? Ask clarifying questions until the feedback is specific enough to act on. You could say, for example, "Thanks! What specifically do you advise me to do differently?" Or you could try to understand the context better by asking, "In which meetings and in which way do you see me not being active enough?" Or simply ask for an example to make it more concrete. Of course, if you were messaging with your partner, looking at the news or the weather forecast, and that's the reason for the feedback, the feedback is accurate and prudent, and there is nothing more to say than something like, "Point taken."

Step Two: Add Your Views or Interpretations

Next, after doing your best to understand the feedback, *add* your views or interpretations. The feedback giver may not understand the context or may have formed an opinion based on too few observations. Often, the same thing can be interpreted in different ways. So you need to supplement with *your* way of seeing things. To continue with the example about meetings: maybe you think you're supposed to be quiet and humble in the meetings because you're new to your job; maybe you think you're only invited to the meetings for information, not to actively participate; or you think you're not sufficiently knowledgeable to participate in your senior colleagues' discussions. Whatever your views or interpretations, you need to add them to the conversation, as the feedback giver may not know or have any chance to know what you're thinking. Then you can continue a constructive conversation from there.

In that conversation, language matters. The best is to use language that keeps the conversation open and constructive. For example, if there seems to be disagreement, open with an inviting statement like: "Let's work out why we have different ways of seeing this."

Make sure to express yourself in a way that shows what *your* view is, instead of arguing or trying to prove the feedback giver wrong. For example, you can say: "The way *I* see it is . . ." When you express yourself this way, you take responsibility for *your* opinion and don't say that the other person is wrong. And that's important because your aim should be that both of you remain open-minded and keep the conversation going. Avoid making closed statements indicating that the feedback giver is wrong, such as, "*You* are wrong" or "*That's* not correct" or "*That's* unfair." If you express yourself this way, the feedback giver is likely to defend his or her position instead of being open to listening to you.

When the conversation ends, convey some type of closure to the feedback giver that clarifies what you intend to do with the feedback. And always thank the feedback giver. Such a closure is usually short and simple: "I appreciate your feedback and will try to do that next time." Nothing more is needed, just an acknowledgment that you understand and what you will do next with the feedback. If you disagree with the feedback or need to reflect on it before you know what to do with it, that's also entirely fair. Just say so, and then the feedback giver isn't left hanging without understanding what you intend to do.

Step Three: Reflect Alone

After the feedback, it's sometimes valuable to reflect alone. If you get emotional or can't think straight when receiving feedback, it can be tough to stay open-minded. Feedback that hurts may be the truths you *most* need to hear, but that may not be possible to realize or admit during a conversation (even to yourself). It requires reflection.

Or maybe—quite the opposite—the feedback was *not* correct when you think about it. Maybe the feedback giver wasn't sufficiently competent or was biased for or against you. Or there was some other reason why the feedback was not correct.

In the end, you and only you can weigh the feedback you receive and determine its meaning and usefulness for you.

Asking for Feedback

It's not enough to just *receive* feedback, because then you won't get enough. You should also actively *seek* it. Ask for it. If you don't ask for feedback on your own initiative, you may not get any, or only a little, because many people don't like giving it (and frankly, many are not very good at giving feedback).

So, why don't people give enough feedback? Well, many people think they're too busy. Others are afraid of hurting people's feelings. Or they worry that they'll get into an argument, or it'll become awkward or uncomfortable. Or they believe they shouldn't interfere, and it's the manager's (or somebody else's) job to give feedback. Whatever the reason, the result is that the feedback stays in people's heads. But, by actively *asking* them, you give them an opportunity, a license, to give you feedback. You turn the situation around and make it easier for the other person. If you're new at your workplace, that gives you an extra opportunity: people *expect* you to ask questions and ask for feedback. Make the most of that opportunity.

When asking, also ask for what you do *right*; don't just ask for what to develop and change. Many people forget or avoid giving this type of feedback. Or they believe that you already know, so they don't have to say it. But it's essential for you to also know what you do *right*, not just what you should correct or stop doing. It's perfectly legitimate to ask for it.

So, how exactly do you *ask* for feedback? Use the following three techniques as a guide:

1. Ask for feedback that is directed toward the *future*. Discussing only what happened in the past is likely to focus on failures and weaknesses and not give you information on *how to improve*. So seek feedback that has a helpful balance between past and future. And let the past contribute with *examples* of what you could change in the future. It's also nicer to discuss what you can improve in the future rather than past failures.

2. Ask for *advice* rather than critique. For solutions rather than problems. Ideas on how to improve rather than comments on what happened in the past. You need feedback to focus on *changes* you can make— otherwise, it's useless. You can ask, for example, "Can you give me some advice on what I can *do better?*" instead of "What do I do wrong?" That way, you have a better chance of getting useful advice that you can put into practice.

3. Ask for *specific* feedback. For example, don't ask, "What do you think of me?" or "Do you have some feedback for me?" That's vague and gives the person you ask no clue what you're after. Instead, ask about a specific skill or task: "When I [do some task], how can I improve?

Is there anything I should do that I'm not doing?" or "I'd like some feedback *on how I . . .*" That's much more specific. Ask clarifying questions until you have specific enough information for you to act on.

If you want to make it even simpler, you can ask for just *one thing* to focus on. That makes it very easy for the person you ask. For example, you can ask, "What's one thing that I can do better?" or "When I [do some task], what's just one thing I can improve?" or "Can you give me just one good piece of advice about [some task]?" (Most people *love* to give a good piece of advice.)

You can also set yourself up to get regular feedback (outside of formal performance reviews). For example, you can set up regular (weekly, biweekly, monthly, or quarterly) sessions with people you work closely with (colleagues, project members, customers). This will not only help you build a habit of seeking and using feedback but it will also help you build important relationships.

Finally, it matters *who* you ask. Feedback should be *accurate.* Otherwise, it's not helpful. That's the key criterion when selecting who to ask. So you should ask those who are most qualified to give you accurate feedback on what you seek to improve. You also want feedback to be *honest,* and that means you want people you believe will be honest with you, even if the feedback may be upsetting. Avoid asking people who don't want to hurt your feelings or are too uncomfortable or conflict-averse to tell you what they think. Ask people who are not afraid of asserting themselves. Counterintuitively, the fastest way to learn and grow is to ask people you instinctively would *not* like to ask: those with whom you have difficulties, those who seem most critical of you, those with whom cooperation *isn't* smooth or dialogue *isn't* good. Find the courage to have a talk and find out what it's really about. Those people are likely the ones who are not afraid of telling you (their version of) the truth and will give you self-insights that you could not have received any other way.

SKILL 2

SETTING GOALS

- Explore and stay open to opportunities.

- Acknowledge your work values. They will guide you to the right work.

- Seek out the people who can give you energy, challenge you, and inspire you.

How do you find out which types of jobs you should strive for? What goals should you aim for? How do you get started on the right path?

At the beginning of your career, a great principle is to *explore and experiment*. You probably want to use the hard skills you've received from your education, but it's difficult to know which exact jobs and roles fit you until you have substantial work experience. It's like before you have tasted something new, you don't know if you like it or not. It might look good but taste awful, or look bland but taste great. Consequently, it's important to do experiments with different jobs, roles, or tasks to learn more about yourself, and to be open to new opportunities and alternatives whenever they offer themselves. Yes, even when it scares you or you feel inadequate. Taking on roles outside of your comfort zone is always going to give you new insights and broaden your view.

Think of it as a process instead of a fixed career result you have to reach. See the start of your career as a series of steps to *discover* more about yourself, work life in general, and potential career paths. With every step, as you gain more experience and discover more skills, you adjust your vision and direction. The more experience you get, the richer your knowledge pool will be when you make your longer-term career decisions. Then, later in your career, when you have tried out a number of different jobs and roles, you'll better know which types of work are a good fit for you, and which are not.

To discover your career path, avoid making a *too* rigid vision for where you want to be in three, five, or ten years. Because with a rigid vision, you risk closing yourself off from many opportunities. It makes sense to have long-term *aspirations*; that's all good. But planning your career in too much detail and too long in advance could work against you. Don't say to yourself, "I have to be X in five years and Y in ten years." Be more open and flexible; such goals are often unrealistic and may blind you from otherwise great opportunities that just don't fit a rigid idea of an ideal career. Instead, say to yourself, "My *current* goal is X" and don't be afraid to change it. Let your goals *emerge* from your experiences instead of trying to *fit* your experiences to your goals. This is also where your self-awareness helps you navigate. Also, recognize that most people have hiccups and detours in their careers, which isn't necessarily bad because they may be the inspiration for entirely new and refreshing directions. What initially seems like a wrong path may be where you end up spending most of your career—and be very satisfied!

So, if it's not five or ten years, then how far out in the future should you make plans? In most cases, you shouldn't make career plans for more than eighteen months into the future. Even as little as six months may be right. With such a relatively short planning timeline, you can keep things flexible. Then, focus on doing your current job as well as you can. Exciting opportunities often go to the best performers and those who show initiative; they are not randomly distributed. Consequently (and ironically), one of the best "planning" strategies is to actually *not* plan too far out in the future but to focus on doing your current job very well.

Of course, being open to opportunities doesn't mean being uncritical and taking just any opportunity that pops up. You still want to exercise control over your career. Instead, when faced with new opportunities, pause and *think*, "Is *this* really what I want?" It may very well be, or it may not.

Similarly, be rational about the advice you get from others when making career decisions. You probably have people around you who are eager to give you recommendations, such as your parents, family and friends, people in your network. And they usually *do* have the best intentions. But what worked for *them* may not work for *you*. If they have other personalities, strengths, and values than you, then their advice may be wrong for you instead of right. And making career decisions to please others or live up to others' expectations isn't the right way to make critical personal decisions. Don't let yourself get talked into something that doesn't feel right. Your goals must come from within. While you should listen to other people's advice, the *decision* is yours.

For example, suppose you are a nurse, and you have a friend who is passionate about working as a trauma nurse and tries to talk you into it. Your friend thrives in the unpredictable and high-stress environment of emergency rooms. But you prefer a calmer work setting and doubt that you would fit in the ER's chaotic environment and believe that specializing in diabetes or oncology might be more like you. Then—although your friend is enthusiastic and well-meaning— you should probably think twice before following your friend's example.

Focus on Your Natural Strengths

To make the most of who you are, focus your energy on your areas of natural strengths instead of weaknesses. When you work within the boundaries of your natural strengths, you're in your *strengths zone*. Obviously, focusing on your strengths zone requires that you first understand what your natural strengths are. Some tips on that were given in Skill 1: Building Self-Awareness. This is an ongoing (discovery) process. As you gain more experience, you'll discover more natural strengths that you didn't know you had. Especially when you challenge yourself outside of your comfort zone.

You want to spend relatively more time and energy in your strengths zone. When you're selecting new tasks, projects, and assignments, you should gravitate toward your strengths zone. That's where you should prioritize improving, and that's where you should set the highest demands for your performance. Train yourself and add new knowledge and skills *first* within your strengths zone. Also, discuss with your manager how to get more work in your strengths zone. That way, you're cultivating the best of yourself. That shouldn't be too difficult, as your strengths zone is where you learn the easiest, perform the best, and enjoy working the most.

Now, remember the discussion about the school system in the Introduction? The school system evaluates you on the *full* curriculum, whether the topics are in your strengths zone or in your weak areas. So, just to keep up, the school system forces you to focus on your weak areas; otherwise, you may not pass exams. But work life is *not* the school system, and a career is *not* a fixed curriculum. On the contrary, you have full control and can construct your own "work curriculum": your career. You can spend less energy in your weak areas and instead spend it in your strengths zone. That's a great deal!

So focus on your natural strengths and consider your weaknesses as only *limitations*. Of course, that doesn't mean you should never spend energy repairing your weaknesses—you sometimes should. But it's a matter of priority. You should *first* focus on your natural strengths and second on improving your weaknesses.

Think about restaurants. They're all specialized: Mexican, Chinese, Cajun, pizza, fine dining, cheap eats, etc. You would probably be suspicious of a restaurant that claimed it did *everything* well. Because you know that it would be a lie or that the owner was delusional. It's the same thing with people: we're good at some things, and people love and respect us for *them*. And as long as we spend most of our time in our strengths zone, it doesn't matter so much what we are not good at. Think about people you admire: they all have weaknesses, but you admire them anyway for their strengths. Nobody has no weaknesses; everybody has many things they're not good at.

But how do you then avoid or minimize negative impacts of your weaknesses?

First, *seek jobs* that play to your natural strengths. As long as enough of what you do is within your strengths zone, you're okay because your weaknesses diminish in relative importance (you'll still have to improve any relevant weaknesses, though). Conversely, if you're in a job that doesn't play to your strengths but to your weaknesses instead, it's time for a change. Look for another job, or try to significantly redefine your job content in collaboration with your manager.

Second, *seek teams* where the team members complement each other. Then your weaknesses can be canceled out by the other team member's strengths. So, when possible, team up with others who have strengths in your weak areas so you can stand strong *together*.

Finally, you can use different aids to help *compensate* for your weaknesses. For example, if your spelling is weak, use spellcheckers or writing apps or have someone proofread what you write. If you're forgetful, use calendar apps and reminders. Whatever your weaknesses are, try to figure out if there are some aids or techniques that can help you compensate.

Discover Your Work Values

Work values are *why* you work. They are your prime source of motivation for working, your way of feeling successful and fulfilled. They are also deeply personal. Work psychologists have categorized work values into three groups:

1. **Money, security, and status:** In this group, people's main motivation is to get income to sustain themselves and their families. Job security is also important, as this group values a predictable income from a steady job. They also appreciate the social status and power they get from a well-respected job or from working for a prestigious organization. This is the conventional definition of "success."

2. **Social connection:** In this group, the main reason for working is the social connections. The social relationships and the sense of "we" mean a lot to people in this group. They enjoy building social bonds and being part of the culture at their workplace. They relish the emotional support people can give each other in times of stress or crisis. They enjoy creating something together with others, which has a higher meaning than the individual. In essence, this group highly values working with other people, regardless if they are colleagues, partners, clients, patients, or customers.

3. **Self-expression:** In this group, people are motivated by the work content. People express themselves through their work. In its purest form, people would work just because they find it meaningful and exciting—as long as their basic needs are met. For example, some find meaning in working with causes of greater common significance like humanitarian, political, or environmental issues. They like an intellectually stimulating job where they can use their strengths and creativity. Many prefer to have a lot of autonomy and freedom to behave and think independently. This group also loves to try out new things and develop themselves professionally and personally.

Notice that when work values are defined in these three categories, it becomes a broader and more inclusive definition of "success." The conventional definition, where success can be *externally* seen and rated, is more comprehensive here, as it includes feelings of success that originate from *within*. It is this—broad and inclusive—definition of "success" that we are using in this book.

Most people will prefer one of the work values over the two others. For some, working with others is the most important—they would hate working alone. Working with others is more important to them than having a prestigious job or working with something of their particular interest. For others, working on something they are passionate about is all-important; they don't necessarily need to work with others or have a high income. And for some, to create a comfortable life for themselves and their families and develop status in society is more important than the other values. Think about what people do if they win the lottery: some people will stop working, and others won't.

All work values are fair and valid. No one value is "better" or more acceptable than the others. For instance, if you don't feel like pursuing a prestigious career, that's perfectly fine. No one should or can define your values for you. Values are, by definition, a personal thing; they represent what is important to each of us in our work. And those values differ a lot. The critical point is to *be true to* your work values. People who find themselves in jobs that *conflict* with their work values are at risk of being unhappy or stressed.

For example, suppose your principal work value is self-expression, and you are demotivated because what you're doing bores you; thus, salary, benefit, or prestige will do little to make you satisfied. Or, suppose your principal work value is money, security, and status, and you get minimal of that; thus, you'll feel dissatisfied even in an exciting job or a job with positive social connections.

In reality, it's likely that you won't yet have a clear understanding of what your work values are. Work values *emerge* and become clearer as you get more experienced. And they change over time. So if you don't know what is most important to you, don't worry; you'll get more clarity with time. Indeed, it's common to prioritize money and security at the beginning of your career when you establish yourself and really need the money. Later in your career, other work values may take higher priority. What's important is that you don't *compromise* on your work values for too long. If you don't get satisfaction and energy from your work, you may end up unmotivated and bitter.

Follow Your Interests—but Not Too Narrowly

Your interests can also give you directions for your career. Identifying your interests isn't too difficult. Simply reflect on what you do when deciding for yourself what to spend your time on. It's what you *spend your time on* that counts—not what you *say* your interests are. For example, what topics do you enjoy discussing with friends and colleagues? Which blogs and websites do you read (or which particular sections)? Which people, companies, and news do you follow? What do you subscribe to? Which nonfiction books do you read? When working (or studying), which activities do you spend extra time on because you're genuinely interested? These are all hints to what your interests are.

Interests are less important than work values when it comes to guiding your career. That's because you don't want to compromise on your work values in the long run. If your work values are severely compromised, it doesn't matter that you work with something that interests you. Additionally, interests are more short-term and fluid in nature than values. Interests come and go; you are not *born* with an interest in something concrete, like neurosurgery, cattle farming, or logistics. Instead, interests are *developed*. Things that don't particularly interest you right now can be developed into interests, especially when you work in your strengths zone. Interests often develop quite by themselves as a result of working with something. So the better you get, and the more competent you feel, the more interested you will be.

And that is extremely useful in the workplace. Because one thing is for sure: there will be lots of change! Technologies, concepts, systems, and regulations change all the time, and if you're *interested* in what you're doing, you'll be more engaged and more persistent and will find your work more joyful. Think about it: if you're genuinely interested in something, you have more fun, try harder, and apply more creativity, which is the recipe for succeeding. And you will be more resilient if something isn't going right. Interests fuel energy and persistence.

That's why you should think of interests as moldable—something you have an active role in controlling. You are not *born* with interests; they develop from experiences. So when you encounter a new challenge, you can think: "That might be interesting. I'll give it a try." When you start working with it, odds are that you'll develop an interest. Especially if new challenges are within your strengths zone and in harmony with your work values, you'll be able to develop interests in entirely new areas. So keep an open mind to new opportunities and challenges. It might turn out that you find them really interesting!

On the other hand, don't insist that you have to be interested in something before even trying it. That way, you avoid closing your mind to opportunities that really *are* attractive if only given a chance.

Get Started Right

So, how *do* you start your work life off on the right track? So far, you know that you should:

- care about your career instead of going with the flow
- take control and make your own decisions
- explore and stay open
- follow your natural strengths
- be true to your work values
- use your interests as guides, but also be open to developing new interests

Further to those principles, some concrete strategies can help you navigate the start of your career.

Pick the Right Workplace

First (and no surprise), finding the right place to work matters a lot. Getting into a good workplace is a priority because you take shape from it. You will unavoidably be a product of the people you work with and network with. You will learn and adapt their strategies, routines, habits, techniques, standards, values, attitudes, manners, behaviors—whether right or wrong, professional or unprofessional. Consciously or unconsciously, you are learning how to do things. And as you have so much to learn when starting your career, it's crucial to work for an organization where you learn the right things, not the wrong things. The start of your work life is as much a *learning experience* as it is a job.

For that reason, one good strategy is to go for jobs where you know that you will *learn* the right things, and prioritize that over short-term goals such as salary or quick promotions. So when choosing your first job(s), deliberately look for organizations where you'll be learning something that sets you up for success *later* in your career. That may require you to do some years of hard work in less-rewarding roles, but that's often the entry ticket into the best organizations. In return, these organizations will teach you the underlying skills that will make you successful later. Said in another way: when you choose a job, ask yourself, "If I take *this* job, how does it affect what my *next* job can be?" That puts you on the track toward your long-term aspirations.

Don't fall for the myth that by working in a bad workplace, you at least learn how *not* to do things. Understanding failure isn't going to help you much. You are not learning how to do things right just by understanding how they are done wrong. How to do things right is not the *opposite* of how to do things wrong! For example, if you're a cook, you will not learn how to make a perfect hollandaise sauce in a kitchen where your colleagues "cook" by heating ready-made food. So if you find yourself in an unprofessional or low-standard environment or in a toxic culture, then it's better to find another job where you learn how to do things *right*.

When looking for the right place to work, don't just go for the hard-skills part of the job. Soft skills are equally important, so include the organization's culture and values in your criteria. Culture and values differ *greatly* between organizations, and you have to fit in and feel good. So before you accept a job, try to understand these things from publicly available sources, from the interview process itself, or from someone who works there (or someone who knows someone who works there).

Pick the Right Manager (if You Can)

Second, your direct manager matters a lot. Ideally, you want a manager who is genuinely interested in you and invests his or her time in your progress and success—a manager you trust and respect and have a good relationship with. Admittedly, that's *not* a given thing; managers come in all shapes and sizes. It's the exception that you have the luxury of choosing your manager; typically, it's the manager choosing you, not the other way around. Or you simply *get* a new manager because your current manager is moving on to another job. But the point is that when you *do* have some choice about who your manager is, it *is* an important criterion. This is also why some people choose to *follow* their manager onto new job positions, if they have a good manager they trust and work well with. Strong manager-employee relationships often last for many years because the need for trust and respect goes both ways.

Change, if a Job Is Wrong for You

Third, be prepared to make changes if you experience a significant job misfit. Workplaces differ enormously regarding professionalism, values, and leadership. And if you make a mistake and accept a job that's plain wrong for you, it's better to move on. Too many people stay too long in jobs that are misfits solely to avoid the challenges and discomfort of changing.

As a rule of thumb, stay at least three months in a new job before concluding that it's not for you. After three months, you'll have a bit of experience to base your decision on, and you'll have had time to make a few successes for yourself. On the other hand, don't wait more than six months in a job you feel bad about before you start looking for another. That should be sufficient time to know that it isn't going to get better or that there are no other attractive career paths for you within that job.

So, how do you know if a job is a misfit or not?

First, talk with someone about your situation. Talk with someone who has more experience than you and can help put your case in perspective. Or speak with some friends: what do *they* experience at *their* workplaces? What difficulties and disappointments have *they* faced? Talking with other people gives you a reality check to better weigh if your expectations are realistic.

But also consider if *you* might be too quick in concluding that your job is a misfit. You may have unrealistic expectations you need to manage and bring to a more realistic level. Or you may have to accept working with people who are more different from you than you're used to. Since some curiosity and openness *are* needed when you start out at a new workplace, you may have to be more flexible than you thought. It's a balance and rarely a black-and-white situation.

SKILL 3

BUILDING CONFIDENCE

- You build confidence by *doing*.

- Making mistakes and feeling uncomfortable is part of learning.

- Be 49 percent realistic and 51 percent optimistic.

Everyone wants confidence. And we can always use more confidence, either to be more confident in skills we already master or to build confidence from scratch in entirely new areas.

First, let's get the definition clear: confidence is what you *believe* you can do. For example, to build a wall with plasterboard or make a sales call. You may believe that you can do both, one of them, or none of them. Thus, *confidence is specific to an activity*. Confidence is the degree to which you believe that the result will be positive when you do an activity. It should not be confused with self-esteem, which is a more general belief one holds about oneself. But there is a fundamental connection: the more confidence you gain in different areas, the more your self-esteem grows.

Confidence is essential in both hard and soft skills. Whether you're learning hard skills or the soft skills that this book is all about, building confidence plays a key role. Confidence benefits you in three ways:

1. **Results:** With confidence, you create better results because it gives you the personal power to take action, take on more challenging tasks, and be more productive.

2. **Resilience:** Confidence makes you more resilient because it acts as a buffer against negative emotions—the more confident you are, the quicker you will be to take action and bounce back from setbacks and frustrations.

3. **Effect on others:** Confidence is interpreted very positively by others; when you're confident, people will think you're competent and successful within that domain—often more than you actually are.

Most soft skills are also *social* skills, and learning social skills sometimes makes people anxious. However, this is completely normal, and most (if not everyone) will admit to being anxious in some social situations. The good news is that there's a proven method to increase confidence, which social psychologists have tested in hundreds of experiments. That's the topic of this chapter.

You Build Confidence by *Doing*

Obviously, our thinking influences what we do. That's how we normally function: we think about something, and then we do it. But it also works the other way around: what we *do* influences what we *think*. Attitudes also follow behavior, which means that you can regulate your thinking and beliefs by what you *do*.

This simple but powerful mechanism is the foundation for building confidence: you build confidence, indirectly, by *doing*. But it doesn't work the other way around: you don't gain confidence just because you, or a friend, or your mother tells you that "you can do it." If you don't think so *yourself*, it has little or no effect. You cannot change simply by deciding to change. Your brain has to believe it. It needs proof.

And *proof* is what this method is all about: to build confidence, you lead with action. You have to start *doing* the activities you want to be confident in. Of course, some part of your brain might whisper, "You can't do it." That's the self-doubt. But then you can put those self-defeating thoughts to the test by starting to do those activities in a small way. And as you get better and experience that you actually *can* do something, your brain starts to believe it, and the self-doubts begin to fade. This is also called the confidence/competence loop: as you become more competent, you gain more confidence. And with more confidence, you get the energy and motivation to challenge yourself more and improve your competence yet again. It's a positive spiral. And in this lies another truth about building confidence: it takes effort. There is no shortcut to confidence. Confidence is *earned*—by hard work, practice, and repetition.

Break Big Goals into Smaller Steps

Usually, it isn't the smartest strategy to just throw yourself into the deep end when learning new skills. It might work, but it might also be a disaster (think skiing or driving). Instead, the safer and proven way is to break big or overwhelming goals into more manageable steps. To build competence—and confidence—you have to improve *progressively* and not demand perfection from yourself from the outset.

This is important, as many skills, not just soft skills, are hard to quickly gain competence in. For example, public speaking, tackling conflicts, pitching ideas, receiving critical feedback, having difficult conversations, or negotiating. These are all skills where competence is built in *small steps*. And that takes time and practice. Like physical exercise, you can't expect to lift heavy weights without training. So it's necessary to break such goals into more manageable steps. That way, you can give yourself increasingly difficult challenges until you get to the level of confidence you seek.

Take public speaking as an example. If that makes you anxious, you are not alone. Most people get nervous talking to a group—the larger the group, the more nervous they become. So the way to learn it is to start *small*. Start by speaking to the largest group you feel like talking to without being *too* uncomfortable. That could, for example, be your project team. That's your first step, and you practice in this group until you can speak freely and reasonably confidently in this environment. Then you progress to larger groups, more high-stakes settings, or more formal presentations—in increasingly challenging steps as you get more confident. Notice that the key to improvement at each step is *practice*. The more you practice, the more confident you will become. More is better. And to learn the most, ask for feedback and reflect on how you did. What went right? What could be improved? Feedback and reflection will help you determine what to focus on improving.

It's important not to aim for a perfect result in this process. It *is* a learning process, so it's expected that your performance isn't 100 percent. Think about building confidence as a process going in a desired direction in *im*perfect steps. For example, when making a presentation to someone, you may stammer a bit, make some mistakes, forget something, or appear slightly nervous. And that's okay! Nobody is expecting perfection from someone who's on a learning curve. And perfection is often not needed anyway; you're evaluated for the *value* you're creating, not for perfection. So if a presentation does what it's supposed to do (e.g., communicate the status of your current project), it's of no significance if you don't make a perfect performance.

Also, if you find yourself in trouble or slightly panicking, focus on being mentally *present* instead of drifting off to thinking about negative consequences. If you're in the middle of a presentation, a critical discussion, a sports game, or something similar where it's essential to focus your attention on the present moment, don't start thinking about the dreadful consequences of a mistake or an unpleasant surprise. Instead, focus on the next thing you have to do and *can* do.

For example, suppose you're presenting and make an obvious mistake. Then keep focusing on the next thing you *can* do: correct the mistake and focus on delivering your next point. Don't start thinking, "Argh, this presentation will be a disaster." By simply keeping on track and occupying your mind with the next thing in front of you, you effectively consume your mental capacity on your present activity and, consequently, block it from being filled with anxious thoughts. The sports metaphor for this is "focus on the next play." That is a perfect analogy, because if a player makes a mistake in the middle of a game, it's destructive to start thinking, "Oh, now we'll lose" or "Now I'll be benched for the next game." That's just letting the team down by drifting off into negative thoughts. There are much better winning odds in focusing all one's mental energy on performing well in the next moment.

Finally, make sure to reward yourself when you do well. You can even decide upon a reward before you begin so you know what to look forward to. For instance, set up a reward for "finishing [difficult task]" or "hosting my first project meeting." The reward can be anything meaningful to you, from simply a well-deserved self-compliment like, "Yeah, I made it!" or a nice coffee break, to something special that you want.

Accept Uncomfortable Feelings

To build confidence (via the confidence/competence loop), you have to move beyond your comfort zone. But *how much* outside of your comfort zone?

The number one rule is that a step *has to be challenging*. However, you can make the step as small as it takes—as long as you move in the right direction. On the other hand, you don't want to make a step *unreachable*: steps that are *too* far outside of your comfort zone can impair learning if things get too challenging or too scary. Aim for a level where things feel *reasonably difficult*, the "sweet spot" between too easy and too challenging.

It's also necessary to be *specific* about what you'll do. If it's vague, it'll be too easy to just stop at your convenience. For example, "I want to speak more in public" is vague. Or, if it's too far out in time, it'll be easy to put off because you believe you can always do it later. For example, "I'll make a presentation for my department in the next half year" is too far out in time. Whereas, "I will ask my manager on Monday if I can make a five-minute presentation on the status of my project at the next department meeting" is both specific and soon, making it sufficiently challenging.

When moving outside of your comfort zone, you'll often feel uncomfortable feelings like anxiety, fear, insecurity, and vulnerability. But if you don't move beyond your comfort zone, you're limiting your development to the confines of what you're comfortable with. You could say that your comfort zone becomes your cage. So you *will* have to accept a certain level of uncomfortable feelings. Some people are okay with that; some even get energized from living on the edge. And others dread it. Whichever type you are, it's still the same cause/effect that's working: development requires moving beyond your comfort zone and accepting some temporary, uncomfortable feelings.

Fortunately, uncomfortable feelings aren't just bad news. Low or moderate levels of anxiety or stress are normal in many situations where one has to perform (and care about the result). Like an exam or a test: as long as the anxiety or stress is not *too* high and becomes counterproductive, it energizes you and increases your attention. The same goes for any type of hard or soft skill. The right level of uncomfortable feelings makes you rise to the occasion. The feelings are not harmful; they're just unpleasant.

The key is, simply, to *accept* that the feelings *are* there. Don't run away from them; *stay* with them through a challenging experience or situation. Then, when you're past your experience, you will have trained your brain—a bit more—to recognize that the "dangerous" feelings are not so dangerous after all. And the way to do that is to stay with your uncomfortable feelings. You'll get more and more used to them, and they'll automatically diminish little by little as you build confidence. Or, as a proverb says, you become "comfortable being uncomfortable." For example, if you feel anxious when presenting in an important meeting, you can accept that this emotion is natural and that you cannot do anything about it right now. Don't fight or dismiss or try to control the feeling; just accept that it *is* there and carry on and make your presentation *while still feeling anxious*. Because when you accept your feelings, you're spending less attention on them. The uncomfortable feelings *are* there, which is okay.

Use this technique for any potentially uncomfortable situation, like stating an unpopular (but necessary) opinion, asking for help, admitting mistakes, giving critical feedback, facing a conflict, etc. And be proud of yourself every time. Because moving beyond your comfort zone and staying with your uncomfortable feelings is *courage*. So, whenever you choose to be courageous, you choose freedom over feelings that would otherwise limit you.

Procrastination

Sometimes the expectation of considerable discomfort can lead you to (unproductively) procrastinate things that you need to do. You procrastinate to avoid uncomfortable feelings.

Procrastination is a shortsighted strategy because you don't get the opportunity to test your self-doubting thoughts and (probably) find out that what you feared wasn't as dangerous or difficult as you thought. Procrastination is postponing discomfort into the future, but at the expense of not getting your self-doubting or anxious thoughts *dis*confirmed by *doing* whatever you feel uncomfortable about.

A simple method to beat procrastination is to decide in advance on a *specific situation* that you might put off or "forget" to do. Instead of saying to yourself, "I have to do it soon" or "I'll do it sometime this week" (which are both vague), make it clear exactly *where*, *when*, and *how* you will do it.

For example, if you're going to have a potentially uncomfortable conversation with a colleague, make a *specific* commitment to yourself: "Tomorrow morning, right after the project meeting, I will go immediately to Liza's office and have that conversation. I will start the conversation by saying X." That way, you have specified *where* and *when* (tomorrow morning, right after the project meeting) and *how* to do it (I will go immediately to Liza's office and have that conversation. I will start by saying X). Once you have decided on "when, where, and how," play it out in your mind visualizing how it will go. This method is effective because when you encounter the situation you specified, your brain will automatically initiate your response so you cannot put it off. The better you imagine and visualize the situation in advance, the better the method works.

Notice that the few moments before doing things that make you uncomfortable are the most unpleasant, but once you get started, you usually feel better. So an essential technique in beating procrastination is to *focus on overcoming the first step*. As soon as you begin the activity, you can concentrate on that instead of the discomfort. To get started, it also helps to accept that *any* action is usually better than *no* action.

For example, let's assume you have to write a difficult email—maybe an email you know will make other people disappointed or angry. In that situation, it's better to get started writing *something* rather than completely postponing it. You could start by making an outline and not aim for the final, polished email. Just make a draft you can continue working on. That takes the pressure off getting started.

Beating procrastination is a gift to yourself. When you stop procrastinating, you spare yourself the nagging thoughts of what you're putting off. These thoughts intrude on, and subtract from, your pleasure and satisfaction of what you're accomplishing.

Mistakes

Making mistakes is part of working. Or, more precisely, part of living. No one can avoid making mistakes. And when you move beyond your comfort zone, you naturally produce *more* mistakes. Consequently, challenging your comfort zone means, at the same time, choosing to make (at least some) mistakes. That's unavoidable. Actually, if you make *no* mistakes, you may be going with too much safety, spending too much time, and taking too little initiative. You're not pushing your comfort zone.

Let's be clear: nobody likes to make mistakes. They may be embarrassing or may hurt others—they have consequences, after all. Sending confidential information to the wrong person, choosing a bad option, making a serious miscalculation, sending incorrect information to customers, misdiagnosing or giving wrong treatments to patients, causing an accident, spilling food, forgetting an important meeting, making a dumb investment—the list is endless. However we look at it, mistakes are no fun. Sometimes mistakes just feel terrible. The trick is to *acknowledge* the feelings of frustration, disappointment, or embarrassment. And move on. You don't want to get stuck in negative speculations and worries.

But *how* do you do that?

The first thing is to *learn* from your mistake: you want to make sure you improve. The culture in most organizations accepts that people make mistakes, but it also expects everyone not to make the *same* mistake twice. To improve, you need to understand what *led to* the mistake. And to make sure that you don't do it again, you want to analyze what happened and figure out what you can do to prevent it from happening in the future. For example, imagine that while you were drafting an email, you accidentally sent it. Unfortunately, the mail was written in anger and included language you intended to delete. To ensure that you never make *that* mistake again, you could change the order of what you do and only add the recipients as the last step when you're satisfied that the mail is ready to be sent. Or, if you went way over your time with a presentation, you'll want to make sure that you're better organized in the future—for example, by adding some buffer time or setting a timer.

The next thing is to *accept* that you'll make mistakes, as they're part of learning. Nobody expects you to make *no* mistakes. That would be impossible. You have to climb the unavoidable learning curve. When you think about it this way, mistakes become *feedback*; they become stepping-stones to success. That's the productive way to frame mistakes.

Finally, it matters *how you speak to yourself* when you make mistakes or fail to accomplish something. When something goes wrong, some people exaggerate the causes and the consequences. That may be in a moment of frustration, but it could also be a self-critical *habit* that produces overly pessimistic explanations. Especially if you tend to be self-critical, use the following three questions to evaluate a situation when you make a mistake or fail at something:

1. Is it "always" or "not always"?
2. Is it "everything" or "not everything"?
3. Is it "me" or "not me"?

Let's assume you just came out of a meeting where you tried to convince a group of people to support a new project. During the meeting, you made some mistakes and got a critical question you couldn't answer. The group didn't show much interest, and they hurried away to their next tasks. Argh! Now it's easy to deem *yourself* incompetent, *always*, and regarding *everything*. For example, to say, "I can never influence anyone about anything" or "I'm no good at this job" or something similar. But let's use the three questions to analyze this situation:

1. **"Always" or "not always"?** Okay, *that particular* meeting didn't go as you had hoped. But when you think about it, you *have* been convincing in many other situations where people were indeed interested! Check "not always."

2. **"Everything" or "not everything"?** You made some mistakes during the meeting, and you couldn't convincingly answer that question. But otherwise, the meeting went fine. So your mistakes don't make you incompetent with *everything*! Check "not everything."

3. **"Me" or "not me"?** There could be entirely different explanations for the group's lack of interest. Perhaps they were stressed out with something urgent and couldn't focus on your topic. Or they simply don't need the project you were trying to convince them about, so your performance wouldn't change anything, whether it was excellent or poor. Thus, you cannot conclude that it was *you* who caused their seeming lack of interest. Check "not me."

Of course, sometimes you do make mistakes, which *are* your responsibility: a clear case of "me." Then, indeed, you *should* assume responsibility—and not blame others or external circumstances. But still: remember that assuming responsibility doesn't mean you're always failing with everything. Yes, you made some mistakes, but no, they're not character flaws. Don't explain your mistakes by not being smart or talented enough. If you do that, it's like saying it's you as a *person* who failed—when, in reality, it was your *performance* that failed.

Instead, when you make mistakes, *analyze* your performance: what went wrong? Did you put enough effort into it? Did you use the right strategy? Did you prepare properly? For example, if we assume that it was, in fact, *you* who failed in that meeting, then analyze what you did wrong. Maybe the mistakes you made weren't the problem at all; maybe the problem was rather that you made your presentation too technical so your audience didn't understand much. Then you have something to improve next time. You can turn this analysis into new motivation and make it your challenge to connect better with your audience next time. This is the ultimate way to make the most from mistakes: understanding their true causes and learning from them.

Perseverance

To build confidence, you often need to keep going, even when things get tough. You have to continue working despite difficulties or discouragement. And although perseverance doesn't guarantee success, success is usually not possible without it. If people gave up quickly, most big companies, sports stars, performers, and politicians wouldn't be what they are. Society definitely wouldn't look the same. Perseverance is a critical ingredient in confidence because *hard-earned* results make your confidence grow more than results that come easily.

But how do you keep going instead of giving up? There are several elements to that.

The first is to use good old-fashioned willpower. *Self-control* and discipline are necessary when problems or discomfort seem unmanageable. Because then it's easy to lose motivation and come up with all kinds of reasons (excuses) to stop. Instead, rely on self-control—if you don't, you effectively make yourself a slave to your mood.

Take networking as an example: it requires that you sometimes approach people you don't know—or who don't know you—and start a conversation. For many, that's uncomfortable. They feel vulnerable and fear being rejected. They may conclude that the easiest way to handle networking is to just avoid it altogether! But it doesn't have to be that way. Even the shy can do it. The first time may be a bit awkward, and you won't feel confident. But that's where perseverance comes into the picture: even if every time you try to connect with someone doesn't go as you hoped, you always learn a little. And you can use that learning with the next person. The key is not to give up but to use your self-control to give it yet another try.

And in that is a related technique: to capitalize on your momentum. When you're doing something, *keep* doing it and keep the momentum up. That's far easier than stopping and making a cold start later. Let's assume that you're at a networking event, for example, a company event or a conference. Then you shouldn't stop after making the first few connections but continue connecting with new people now that you're warmed up. Or likewise, if you're working with something difficult, don't stop, but keep going and keep focusing when you're first at it. Use your momentum.

The second element is to think *optimistically*. Optimism is thinking about how things might *work* instead of (pessimistically) thinking about what could *go wrong* or what's missing. It's seeing the glass half full instead of half empty. Especially when under pressure, it's helpful to be optimistic, as optimism expands your comfort zone. It makes you work harder and continue for longer, because you have a greater belief that you will succeed. At least some optimism is necessary when trying to do something hard.

But there is a condition to the optimism: it cannot be blind or illusionary optimism; it has to be *realistic optimism*. Naivete or daydreaming isn't going to cut it. Think about it: if you're overly optimistic and believe that something will be easy, you might not put as much effort into it as required. In a high-stakes meeting, if you're unrealistically optimistic and believe that a positive outcome is a sure thing, why prepare much? However, that fantasy may turn into a brutal wake-up call when you realize that it was much more challenging than your unrealistic optimism led you to imagine.

Instead, be realistically optimistic: believe that you will eventually succeed, *and* be realistic about the difficulties you may encounter. Think through the possible obstacles and make realistic assumptions about the risks you face and the mistakes you will likely make. That way, you'll focus not only on how nice it'll be to obtain your goal, but you'll focus on the difficulties ahead too. Let's take the high-stakes meeting example again, but now assume that you are realistically optimistic. Then you'll want to think through what result you aim for and what can go wrong. That result could be: "I want to get the project approved for the next phase." What can go wrong could be: "My presentation isn't convincing; I can't answer their questions; they don't take me seriously because I'm a junior." With those realistic thoughts about what could go wrong in your mind, you'll probably prepare well, have individual conversations with key people before the meeting, prepare answers to critical questions you foresee, etc. In other words, realism makes you *perform* at your best—and optimism makes you *believe* that you can do it.

SKILL 4

BUILDING RESILIENCE

- Focus on what you can control.

- Take a step back and *choose* your reaction instead of reacting reflexively.

- Open up and share with someone you trust.

Everybody will experience frustrations, disappointments, conflicts, and failures at work. Projects run over time and budget, colleagues talk behind your back, you make a grave mistake, your manager treats you unfairly, things break and need fixing when you're most stressed, people complain, problems pile up. The list is long.

Correspondingly, *everybody* will experience negative emotions at work from time to time. Life is inevitably full of ups and downs. But while adversities and unpleasant feelings cannot be avoided, people have different abilities to bounce back; it's the *speed of recovery* that differentiates people. So it's all the more important to understand how you can best recover from adverse events.

This chapter contains some of the best techniques people use to bounce back. What works best for each individual is personal; you may find some of the techniques very useful and others not so much. And that's fine; just use those that make the most sense for you. What's important is that you *do* something about it when you're hit by adversities.

Understand Your Circle of Control

The famous "Serenity Prayer" reads:

> "God, grant me the serenity to accept the things I cannot change,
>   courage to change the things I can,
>   and wisdom to know the difference."

That may be the best resilience advice ever given: some things you simply shouldn't spend energy being frustrated about! Those are the things you have no control over. Because, fundamentally, it's only your *thoughts* and your *actions* that you can control. Your attitude and effort. Everything else is outside of your control.

This concept is called the *circle of control*: what is inside you can control, and what is outside you cannot control.

For example, you have no control over whether your organization is sold, whether a competitor makes a very low bid, whether your project is scrapped in a strategic decision, whether your job is cut to save money, or whether legislation suddenly changes. The same goes for natural disasters, wars, weather, the general economy, pandemics, media, news, etc. These are all events that you cannot influence. The only thing within your circle of control is how you *react* to the events. For instance, if your job is cut to save money, you can react by focusing your energy on how to move on and get a new job. Plus, you can minimize the energy you spend fuming over a decision you cannot influence or reverse. Those (resilient) reactions are entirely within your circle of control.

Other things you can *influence*, but their outcomes are still outside of your circle of control. For example, you can influence other people's opinions, but you cannot control them. Their opinions are their opinions. Or, via your actions, you can influence whether a customer buys or a patient heals, and thus affect the *probability* that things turn out the way you wish. However, there are *other* factors you cannot control, and they can affect the outcome in the opposite direction. For example, if the customer prefers another brand or if the patient doesn't follow the treatment plan when he or she is back home. These factors are outside your circle of control (despite your best efforts to influence the outcome).

Thus, resilience comes from 1) *accepting* what you cannot control and 2) instead *focusing* your efforts on what you *can* control. Let's examine these elements separately:

1. *Accept* **those things you cannot control.** Sometimes things just don't turn out the way you would prefer: your manager is unreasonable, people react negatively, etc. That's just reality, and you have to accept it. Clearly, *accepting* reality doesn't mean you have to *like* it; you obviously have preferences for some outcomes over others. It only means that you know what reality is and recognize that it is what it is. Being offended, angry, or annoyed (non-resilient reactions) will not help. On the contrary, those reactions will make you a less effective problem-solver of things *inside* of your circle of control because you waste your energy in the wrong place.

2. *Focus* **your efforts on what you can control.** By focusing on what you *can* control, you can take responsibility for that and let go of the rest. And what you can *control* is your own actions. For example, while you cannot control how your manager evaluates you, you can certainly *influence* it: you can do your job as well as you can, you can ask for feedback to better adjust to expectations, etc. Such actions are entirely within your circle of control. Or, let's assume that a project you've been enthusiastically working on for the last six months is suddenly closed. Then, once you have absorbed the first disappointment, focus on what to do next and on saving any reusable parts of the now-closed project. Take with you the things you've learned, the ideas you can use in the future, and the relationships you've built. What you *shouldn't* do is get overly upset and spend a lot of time criticizing the decision. That's just prolonging your frustration and is a non-resilient reaction.

In sum, the first thing you should do when hit by adversities is to determine what's inside of your circle of control and what's not. Then direct all your efforts toward the constructive actions within your control. And waste as little energy as possible on the things you cannot influence or change.

Understand Your Automatic Thoughts

Automatic thoughts are those that you're not aware of—they're not based on conscious thinking. They just pop spontaneously into your mind. Most of the time, automatic thoughts serve you well. Imagine driving a car: when you do that, you react more or less automatically to the events in traffic, like red lights or green arrows. You (normally) simply react without deliberation to those events because your automatic thoughts guide you. If they weren't there—like when you were *learning* to drive—driving would be complicated and slow with all that deliberate thinking. Automatic thoughts are 100 percent necessary for humans to be efficient in their daily life.

However, automatic thoughts are sometimes based on experiences or beliefs that are not true or no longer true. But you still *react* as if they were. And that's a problem. For example, if you're used to driving on the right side of the road and travel to a country where people drive on the left side. Then there's a problem if you let your guard down and rely only on your automatic thoughts: you will likely make the mistake of driving on the wrong side of the road.

The principle can be illustrated this way:

Event → Automatic Thought → Reaction (a behavior or an emotion)

Why is this important? Because if you understand that some of your thoughts are automatic, you can intervene. You can *choose* another reaction instead of just reacting reflexively. Instead of just going on autopilot, you can break your habitual patterns of responding. And that's immensely valuable because then you get the *opportunity* to respond in other ways (e.g., responding more calmly and sensibly). Automatic thoughts are just *thoughts* rather than something you *must* react to. It's like the difference between a robot and a human:

a human can think and choose a new response; a robot can only do what it is programmed to do.

Let's assume that a colleague is noticeably grumpy one morning when you come to work. As soon as you notice your colleague's attitude, automatic thoughts kick in. They could be very different interpretations: from "what a jerk" (an angry reaction, you feel violated) or "he must have had a bad morning" (an understanding reaction), to "I must have done something wrong" (a self-critical reaction). The point is that you actually don't *know* why your colleague is grumpy, but your brain automatically picks an interpretation anyway. And you believe that to be the truth and react correspondingly—with anger, empathy, or anxiety. So, if you can intervene and override your first thought with deliberate thinking, you can bring your response inside your circle of control, where it rightly belongs. And that is essential for reacting more resiliently.

Challenge Your Automatic Thoughts

Understanding your automatic thoughts is especially valuable *when you're upset*. When you're upset, you must pay attention to the thoughts and beliefs behind those feelings. Ask yourself what emotions you're feeling: anger, sadness, guilt, anxiety, or embarrassment? What are the *thoughts* causing those emotions? The problem is that when you're upset, automatic thoughts are especially prone to kick in and distort your thinking.

When that happens, you can use the following techniques to help yourself challenge your thinking. The common strategy in these techniques is, simply, to *compare your thoughts with reality*. You can use the techniques just in your head, or you can write your analysis down to better collect your thoughts.

Recognize Thinking Errors

First, it's helpful to understand some common thinking errors. Sometimes we simply *think incorrectly*. Our brains are (unconsciously) playing tricks with us, and as a consequence, we overreact or react wrongly. These "thinking errors" are completely normal—but to the extent possible, you want to recognize them, and correct them. That makes your thinking more accurate and prevents you from overreacting or reacting wrongly. So when you're under pressure or upset, consider if you've made any of these thinking errors:

- **Filtering:** When you make this error, you observe only some information and filter away other information. This is a natural and even necessary process; without it, you would be overloaded with information. But sometimes, the wrong information is filtered out, which distorts your perception of reality. You get tunnel vision: you focus on something and ignore the rest (which could be the most important). For example, let's say you think someone is rude. Then you will be acutely aware of any of this person's behaviors that *support* your belief. But when the person does something that does *not* support that belief, your brain could catch it in the filter and *not* make that information available to you—for instance, an act of courtesy. That way, you (incorrectly) build up your belief that the person is rude.

- **Jumping to conclusions:** When you jump to conclusions, you guess or assume things you don't have enough information about, which can lead you to form random opinions that may be completely false. For example, if your manager asks you to see him or her in the office the following morning, you may jump to the conclusion that you're going to have an unpleasant conversation about a mistake or a complaint. But, in fact, you don't *know* that. That's just your inference. It may be something completely different and entirely positive that your manager wants to talk with you about.

- **Mind reading:** This is a variation of jumping to conclusions where you believe that you know what other people are *thinking*. But, of course, you don't *know* what they are thinking. For example, that may lead you to believe that a rude person doesn't like you or is critical of you. But, in reality, the person's rudeness could be just a bad habit that has absolutely nothing to do with you. You may just be taking it personally with your (incorrect) mind reading.

- **All-or-nothing thinking:** When you make this error, you think categorically; people or things are either "good" or "bad," "stupid" or "smart," "hardworking" or "lazy," etc.—but nothing in between. It is either black or white, with no shades of gray. This error is harmful because it'll make you judge people or things in categorical terms, which is seldom correct. It's much more realistic, for example, to see people as complex and emotional beings with strengths and weaknesses, good and bad days, and so on. People are not just two extremes of a scale. And that goes for yourself as well: if you're prone to all-or-nothing thinking, you will evaluate *yourself* in equally unforgiving ways as either "perfect" or "failure." That is not only erroneous thinking, but hurtful self-evaluation.

How Would You Talk to a Friend in the Same Situation?

One of the simplest ways to check if your thoughts are accurate is to consider how you would talk to a friend in the same situation. That way, you step out of your upsetting situation to get an outside-in look at it. Let's say your manager receives a complaint about you from a customer, patient, or colleague and you jump to the conclusion that "my career is in danger" and cannot stop thinking about it. Then you can consider what you would say to a friend who has this problem. You can also imagine that you are a detective or a scientist trying to get to the objective truth about what happened. For example, you can ask your "friend" the following types of questions:

1. What is the *evidence for* the thought "My career is in danger"? The answer could be: the evidence is that one complaint.

2. What is the *evidence against* it? The answer could be: your manager hasn't shown any signs of you being in trouble.

3. What is a *more accurate* way of thinking based on the evidence? The answer could be: the complaint should be taken seriously and dealt with. But it's unlikely to negatively affect my career.

Look for Alternative Explanations

Another technique is to look for alternative explanations. Often, there can be several different explanations for a given situation. However, when your brain interprets the situation, it may quickly pick only *one* of them, making you blind to the other. It's like your brain is completely satisfied now that it has an explanation.

With this technique, you instead *force* yourself to deliberately think about other possible explanations, which can give you a more nuanced picture of what happened. For example, some alternative explanations for a complaint could be: It is baseless or wrong. It is exaggerated. It comes from a person who always complains, so it should not be taken too seriously. The complainer was frustrated about something else but unfairly took it out on you. Thus, by forcing yourself to look for alternative explanations, you can avoid (erroneously) picking the first one that comes to your mind.

Consider if Your Iceberg Beliefs Are Interfering

Remember the negative iceberg beliefs (from Skill 1: Building Self-Awareness): achievement orientation, acceptance orientation, and control orientation. Especially when you're under pressure or upset, iceberg beliefs can interfere with your ability to reason. You may overreact to situations in ways that are predominantly determined by your iceberg beliefs. For example, if your manager gets a complaint about you, you would react in different ways depending on your iceberg beliefs:

- If you are *achievement*-oriented, you would get anxious about your performance and think that your manager will deem you incompetent. You might get defensive or angry.

- If you are *acceptance*-oriented, you would fear that your manager would like you less because of the complaint. You might become apologetic or pleasing.

- If you are *control*-oriented, you may feel shame and blame yourself for not having done enough. But outwardly, you might not show these feelings but instead work obsessively to get "in control" again.

Those are three completely different (non-resilient) reactions to precisely the *same* situation. So if you think your reaction may be affected by an iceberg belief, take a step back and focus on the iceberg belief itself instead of the situation that triggered your reaction. Then you can use the other techniques in this chapter to challenge those iceberg beliefs. Doing so makes you focus on the *real* problem—the iceberg belief—which is the underlying reason behind your response.

Get Perspective on Worries

Worries are thoughts that are all about the *future*. They are about things that haven't happened *yet*. They are about uncertainty, events outside of your circle of control. And for many people, uncertainty is hard to live with. Some would even prefer an unpleasant outcome they know for sure rather than living with the uncertainty. But in a complex environment like work, uncertainty is built in. Some things will not go as you hope. There *is* a possibility of making mistakes and wrong decisions, missing deadlines, being criticized, getting into embarrassing situations, having people reject you, losing your job, etc. But many people overestimate that probability. Or they overestimate the severity of the consequences, which, in turn, makes them worry.

The best way to address worries is to acknowledge the potential consequences. Many people avoid thinking about the *worst* consequences because they dread the unpleasant emotions they would have if the worst should happen. But in reality, you worry less if you dare to think through the possible outcomes, both the good and the bad.

This technique to reduce worrying has three steps.

Step 1: What Is the Worst That Could Happen, and What Would You Do?

If we continue with the example about your manager getting a complaint about you, the *worst* outcome would be to get fired. The (incorrect) thinking could go like this: Your manager starts being critical of you after getting the complaint. As a result, your confidence and performance go down. Eventually, you get fired. This common type of thinking is called *catastrophizing*: taking a relatively minor event and—in one's mind—blowing up the consequences in a chain of bad events:

- complaint → manager starts being critical of you
- manager starts being critical of you → confidence and performance go down
- confidence and performance go down → get fired

The problem with catastrophizing is that it links unlikely events together so that the worst consequences seem much more likely than they really are. But however unlikely the worst outcome may seem, it has to be taken seriously.

The first step is to acknowledge that there *is* a risk (however small) that the worst outcome might happen. In the example, you would have to relate to the idea of being fired and think through that situation: What could you do? What alternative opportunities do you have? How would you search for another job? Even if you hate the idea of this bad outcome, you must find the courage to relate to the worst outcome's real-world consequences and think through how you would cope with that. That's a critical element in reducing the worry, as it gives you tangible ideas on how to cope, where you would otherwise just have a threatening hole of uncertainty.

Step 2: Get Real

In the second step, it's time to gain perspective and come up with something more reasonable than the worst outcome. You must move from being overly influenced by your emotions to more rational thoughts.

First, estimate how realistic the worst outcome *really is*. You do that by estimating the probability of each event in the imagined chain of bad events. But be aware that it must be *realistic* probabilities, so try to step back from your worrying state and estimate a reasonable likelihood of each event. For example, that may look like this:

- Your manager starts being critical. Probability = 5%
- Your confidence and performance go down. Probability = 10%
- You get fired. Probability = 2%

Then multiply these probabilities. In the example, you would get an overall probability of 0.01%. Consequently, you shouldn't waste your mental energy on this scenario.

Instead, now that you've convinced yourself that the catastrophic outcome is highly unlikely, you want to get real and come up with the most *realistic* consequences. For example, a realistic consequence is that your manager will want to talk with you about what went wrong, get your perspective on the situation, and discuss how to avoid it in the future. That's realistic.

Step 3: Focus on What You *Can* Do, Here and Now

Finally, focus your energy, here and now, on what you *can* do about the problem or adversity. What actions can you take now or very soon that address the *most realistic* consequences?

In the example about the complaint, you could prepare for a conversation with your manager. You could investigate the complaint to get a more detailed and objective understanding. You could discuss the case with your colleagues and get their advice. You could consider if you needed some training to do better in the future. And if appropriate, you could reach out to the complainer and discuss the problem. These are all constructive actions you *can* take—here and now. And *taking some form of action* (instead of just worrying) is central to reducing worry!

Distracting Yourself for a While

Sometimes, when you get overwhelmed by emotions and feel unable to think straight or focus, the best you can do, at the present moment, is to distract yourself with something else while you calm down and let yourself find your feet again. That doesn't mean you shouldn't reflect or challenge your thinking as discussed above—only that you *postpone* it for later. Let's say you get angry with a colleague and cannot stop thinking about this person and the situation that created the frustration. Then it's probably wise to go to the gym or take a long walk (or whatever works for you) first before you try to objectively analyze the situation.

Distracting activities can be anything you can think of, as long as it makes you occupy your mind with something else as you cool down. For instance, you can dive into a work task that you know will consume you. Sports activities, singing, and laughing are also good choices because they reduce stress and elevate your mood.

Distracting yourself also works better than trying to *suppress* unwanted thoughts from your mind. After an adverse event, you may repeatedly tell yourself, "I must stop thinking about X." But unfortunately, "thought stoppage" doesn't work. It not only doesn't work, but it also makes the problem worse. Why? Because when you think about a thought in order to stop it, that thought, in itself, contains the thought you want to get rid of! It's a paradox. Instead, it's better to simply *accept* the unwanted thought: "Okay, here's that thought again. I accept that it is here. It will go away at some time. But I am not going to force it to go away." When you do that, the unwanted thought gets less attention, and it fades away as you start occupying your mind with other things.

Use Your Relationships

In addition to what you can do yourself, it's essential to use your relationships. Strong relationships are another key to resilience. Your colleagues, friends, and family can often help you get your thinking on the right track—and even if their advice isn't particularly useful, it often helps just to talk with someone about your problem. Even saying it out loud and formulating it to another person helps your thinking become clearer.

So don't keep your problems to yourself. Share them with trusted others. And don't assume that others know you're having trouble; you might have to say it directly and ask for their support. Even if you feel embarrassed or angry or have other strong emotions, it's better to try to calm down and tell the story. And don't wait for too long. To get the most out of talking with others, dare to speak about your emotions. Dare to be vulnerable, and don't keep your weaknesses or mistakes secret. You may learn that you have much more support and understanding than you thought, even when sharing personal things.

Also try not to *only* talk with people you know will support and comfort you. Because sometimes it's even more important to speak with people who aren't afraid of challenging you and helping you see the situation from another angle or point of view. You may have some automatic thoughts going around in your head that need to be debated or contradicted. That kind of advice and coaching should especially come from people with relevant experience and backgrounds. So dare to also talk with those individuals you know might contradict and challenge you. They may turn out to give you the *best* support.

Finally, resilience is a team sport. Your team (including your manager) is important for your resilience. In a good team, where people have each other's backs, being resilient is something the team is *together*. Something that makes the whole team stronger. But if those relationships are dysfunctional (e.g., there is little trust in the group, and people feel they have to protect themselves against each other), it damages everyone's resilience. That's why one of the best ways to strengthen your resilience is to invest in your important relationships. Behaving reasonably and professionally with your coworkers not only makes you more resilient, but it *prevents* many conflicts and adverse events from happening in the first place. The coming chapters will go through the skills of building these relationships at the workplace. Those skills are immensely important—not only for your performance but also for your resilience.

SKILL 5

PROFESSIONAL BEHAVIORS

- Gain respect with professional behaviors.

- Some behaviors should be avoided at work.

- Follow the expectations for professional etiquette.

In a workplace, people with very different backgrounds and values must work together, which requires them to behave according to certain norms and rules that make interactions as smooth and pleasant as possible. (And frictions and personal conflicts as few as possible.) These norms and rules are often called "professional behaviors."

Professional behaviors are something that everyone can learn, and everyone *should* learn. These behaviors have nothing to do with natural strengths, and their absence can therefore not be excused with the explanation that it's a personal weakness. Behaving *un*professionally cannot be excused by, for example, "that's how I am" or "that's just my style."

You don't have to be brilliant in all the professional behaviors; it's okay to have some not-so-strong areas. In fact, what often matters most is that you *avoid* a handful of *bad* behaviors that are noticeable and frustrating to others. These bad behaviors make you stand out negatively, and that's not what you want. If you realize that you exhibit any of these behaviors, fixing them should be your first priority. For example, if you're aware that you can come across as arrogant, you need to work on this habit first. This is also where feedback comes in as a helpful tool to identify habits and behaviors you need to improve.

Of course, you sometimes meet people who disregard (many of) the professional behaviors or display bad behaviors. Their managers and colleagues may not have the competence or courage to address their problems, or they may *accept* their behaviors—usually because the misbehaving individuals deliver certain results that the organization needs.

But bad behaviors always have consequences—some more visible than others. Individuals who behave unprofessionally may lose their jobs, but the effects are usually less visible. Instead, they may not be getting as exciting or challenging work as others, or they aren't getting salary raises or promotions as quickly as others. Or they simply aren't getting along with anyone—making them *tolerated*, but nothing more. Even less visible are the consequences for the organization's results, which always suffer in the long run.

In any case, even when you're working with people who behave unprofessionally, you must not let *their* bad behaviors inspire *you* to misbehave yourself. Their behaviors are *their* problem. That also goes for managers: just because they're managers doesn't mean they're automatically good role models. Consequently, you must take responsibility for your own behaviors, as they are entirely within your circle of control. You always have the *choice* of behaving professionally. So hold yourself to high standards. Because while lacking professional behaviors hinders your career, mastering them is a great (and highly ethical) way of differentiating yourself and creating a successful work life.

Basic Professional Behaviors

The most basic of professional behaviors are, in a sense, age-old truths. They are universal principles that, when followed, enable human collaboration. They are as much about attitudes and values as they are about the actual behaviors themselves: with the right attitudes and values, the behaviors follow naturally.

Showing Respect

The more you show respect for everyone, the more everyone will respect you back. And you show your respect by doing your best to treat others impartially, without prejudices or biases.

This means that you treat everyone with the same respect and by the same principles, regardless of position. You speak with everyone as equal human beings. This goes for people who occupy positions both lower and higher in the organization than you. Work life is not a zero-sum game where somebody has to lose for you to win. So meet everyone with the same respect and decency. That's likely to be reciprocated.

It also means showing an inclusive mindset and working with everyone regardless of background, education, culture, etc. It means respecting the diversity of the people you work with. You don't want to judge them on anything other than their work contribution.

When it comes to people's individual personalities, it's the same story: everyone has different natural strengths and weaknesses. But that shouldn't affect your respect. Of course, we are naturally more inclined to work with some people than others; we just *click* better with some people. But as a professional, that shouldn't make a difference. Professional behavior is inclusive to everyone, regardless of their personality.

You also treat people most respectfully if you start by assuming that they are doing their best. As humans, we're often quick to judge people we work with. It's easy to deem them incompetent, lazy, disrespectful, or something else, which is usually incorrect. The fact is, we don't *know* the conditions they work under. We don't know what pressure they're under, what priorities they're given, and what else is going on in their lives. Additionally, when we judge others, it often says as much about ourselves as it says about the other person; in fact, our judgments may be projections. That's why it's respectful to base your interactions with other people on the assumption that *they are doing their best*. If you sometimes meet people who *aren't* doing their best, it shouldn't change your initial assumption.

Showing Humility

At work, it's often all too easy to see the deficiencies. It's easy to see the flaws in one's colleagues, and it's easy to see the decisions that, in hindsight, were wrong. All organizations and people have shortcomings. However, as easy as it is to see the *problems*, it usually isn't as straightforward to come up with better *solutions*, or to understand the struggles and hard decisions that formed the organization's history.

That's why humility is the professional starting point. Your workplace has a history—often a long history—that has created its current culture, structure, and processes. And many of your colleagues have long histories—with their own successes, struggles, and disappointments. So, while it may be easy to see necessary and sensible improvements, they may not be feasible. The organization may lack the resources to make those improvements, or it may have other priorities. This isn't to say that you shouldn't try to drive change (you should), but just that it's apt to be humble and respectful of the work and decisions made in the organization before you started. Being humble is a sound starting point for many interactions, and it makes you more receptive to the opinions of others. And less defensive of your own.

Especially when you're new to a job, it can be difficult to assess whether things you observe as peculiar or needing improvement are worth mentioning. For example, you may believe that some software is outdated and needs to be replaced, or that a process is far behind the current best practice. But should you be humble and assume that what you see is based on sound decision-making and shouldn't be questioned? Or should you voice your opinion and risk that you are questioning the obvious?

To solve this dilemma, it's a good tip to write down your observations. Keep a list. Then, after an initial period of employment—for example, the first three months—review the list and remove everything from it that you now know has a good reason for being that way. Finally, share those observations that are left on the list with your colleagues or your manager. That way, your valuable input won't get lost. An outsider's eyes on an organization often reveal things people have gotten used to but, in reality, need to change.

Showing Interest in Others

Showing interest in those you work with positively influences your relationships, making your daily collaborations nicer and smoother. One of the most effective ways of doing that is to learn—and use—other people's names. When you do that, people feel valued. Even if you find it hard to remember other people's names, make an effort. It's a simple thing, but it means a lot!

Apart from using people's names, you can show your interest in numerous ways in your daily interactions by caring to:

- say hello to everyone you meet, including people you don't know
- give a smile
- look at people when they come into a room
- spend a minute socializing first before getting into the matter at hand
- congratulate others on their birthdays
- invite others to join you for lunch
- empathically listen when someone needs it
- show a helping hand when needed

Showing interest tells other people you value them for who they are and not for how they may be useful to you. Showing interest is therefore giving a bit more than what's merely your dutiful respect; it's being kind without expectation or assurance of getting anything in return.

Socializing

Socializing is part of work life, and it's professional to take part in it to show that you're engaged (and hopefully because you enjoy it). It doesn't matter if you're naturally introverted or extroverted, shy or sociable; what matters is that you show up. *Not* showing up sends the signal that you don't care or that you think you're more important than them, or that you don't like them. So it's much better to participate in at least some of the social activities.

Think about it this way: a reasonable level of socializing is *part of* your job, as it builds your relationships and network. Especially when you're new to a job, it's essential to seek out social and informal interactions, as they give you the chance to let your colleagues get to know you—and you them. For example, you can stay ten minutes more after work for a bit of socializing. When people know you better, they'll also instinctively involve you more in their work and interesting projects.

Socializing shouldn't be confused with making friends, though. Of course, genuine friendships *do* evolve from time to time at work, but forming friendships is not the main purpose. Instead, the purpose is to build better and deeper working connections that enable you to work together in a tone of mutual respect, appreciation, and understanding. And while socializing often centers on work, it is also appropriate to be more personal as you get to know people better. So be prepared to reveal something about yourself and your personal life. However, being personal is never inappropriate self-disclosure, so be careful to read the signs of receptiveness of those you speak with. People's limits for what they want to share or know at work are very different.

And yes, socializing involves small talk. That may be about the weather, sports, news, vacation, etc. But it can equally well be about work. And while small talk isn't everybody's favorite, there *is* a point to it: connecting people. So even if you don't like it much, try anyway. There is an enormous difference between trying and not trying. And people will feel that. A tip is to go for conversation topics that you know interest the other person; then he or she will likely be more talkative. Also, to keep the conversation going, use open-ended questions like "What happened next?" or "What did you like most?" Closed questions like "Do you like it?" or "Did you participate in the meeting?" can be answered with a yes or no and thus risk stopping the conversation.

Seeking the Positive

Work life is, almost by definition, a mix of good and bad, success and failure. How you approach this mixed bag has a big say on how happy you'll be with your job. And the attitude that will bring the most joy to your work life is to look for the positive: look for people, things, and accomplishments to enjoy, admire, be grateful for, take pleasure in, or feel elevated by. The more you find that you can appreciate, the more positive you will be, which will show in your attitude and behavior. Positive and appreciative people are like magnets to their colleagues: everybody gravitates toward them. That's a double-win: you will be happier with your work and your relationships will be better. So make it an *active choice* to try to seek out what you like in your job.

Of course, looking for the positive doesn't mean you shouldn't be looking for weaknesses and threats to be addressed—you should. The point is that you want to make sure you have a channel open and are receptive to the positive and inspiring. Because in a hectic work environment, it's easy to get pulled into your work and its everyday struggles. Then it's vital to have an eye on the good and positive to keep oneself balanced.

Expressing Appreciation

Expressing appreciation is one of the basics of making interactions between people smooth and pleasant. It's both simple and powerful. It shows that you appreciate what the other person or group is doing and reaffirms the good feelings between you. It cultivates goodwill and is extremely motivating for those on the receiving end. Appreciation is an unlimited resource that you can tap into again and again; saying "thank you" is quick and doesn't cost you anything.

The best way to express appreciation is to do so immediately and when you *feel* it. Spontaneous gratitude always feels sincere to the receiver, so don't delay it. Do it as soon as possible. Any form is acceptable: verbal, in writing, an emoji, a gift, or whatever.

However, if you feel grateful but fail to express it, the other person doesn't get the pleasure of receiving your appreciation. That's a little like wrapping a gift but never giving it. So when you *feel* grateful, take it as a cue to also *express* it.

Having Fun

Bringing some fun and humor into work lifts spirits and reduces stress. Sharing a good laugh is a great way to feel closer, to feel good together. Humor builds relationships and team spirit, and it can be a means to break the ice, cope with challenging events, or turn around a tense situation.

Of course, humor needs to be dosed with situational awareness: sometimes the *timing* may be wrong for otherwise appropriate humor. For example, when people discuss something serious or concentrate intensely. So tread carefully and try to understand what types of humor seem acceptable before telling any jokes.

Some types of humor are just not fit for work, like malicious humor that diminishes people you work with (ridicule, parody, or mockery). Or humor that is racist, sexist, or otherwise biased. Delivering it as being "just a joke" is not a valid excuse; the unpleasant message still shines through. Humor at work should be inclusive and bring people together.

Being Open to Change

The reality in most organizations is that there is *always* change. New opportunities and threats evolve all the time, and organizations have to adapt. Therefore, they *need* their employees to be open to change; they need people to be curious and routinely unlearn and relearn. The professional attitude is, therefore, to be open-minded and embrace change.

That doesn't mean you should automatically agree to any change, nor that you shouldn't constructively question it. However, it *does* mean that you generally need to have a positive and accommodating attitude toward change. Resisting, ignoring, discounting, or avoiding change will only cause frustration—for yourself and for the organization. Consequently, you have to *relate to* change outside your circle of control. And the best way to do that is with an attitude of curiosity. Then you can take an active part in shaping it.

Bad Behaviors (Not to Bring to Work)

Some behaviors should be avoided at work, and strong hard skills cannot justify or excuse them. These bad behaviors tend to show themselves when people are stressed, under pressure, or outside of their comfort zones—not so much when things are going *their* way and everybody agrees and supports them. They are often connected with negative iceberg beliefs.

The following sections focus on five bad behaviors: passive, aggressive, arrogant, manipulative, and negative. They are unprofessional and create resentment and conflict. To the extent that you recognize yourself in any of them, try to work on them by talking with friends, using a coach, reading books, changing habits, or whatever works for you. But don't be too hard on yourself if the changes you want don't appear as quickly or easily as you would like; it takes time and practice to change behaviors. But it's within your circle of control and well worth it—both for yourself and for others.

Passive Behavior

Some people behave passively because they place their own needs and wants below others. They disregard their own opinions and feelings. And while doing so is sometimes an act of appropriate respect or humility—or just what is fitting in the situation—it's unprofessional if it's a *habit*. If people habitually act passively to fit in or to avoid making mistakes, being criticized, or being embarrassed, they won't contribute their best. Their competencies do not come fully into play. And that's a loss—both for the person behaving passively and for the organization. The school behavior of taking the back seat and staying passive is not what organizations hire people to do; they hire people to *contribute*.

Passive people are also frustrating for those around them, as they'll have to make an extra effort to drag them out of their passivity—an effort they often won't make. Other people may not understand what competencies the passive person has. Thus, a passive person risks becoming overlooked and seen as irrelevant.

Some examples of passive behavior:

- Not stating one's opinions
- Not taking responsibility when critical situations arise and a timely response is needed
- Not giving others feedback, even when it's truly warranted
- Not taking the initiative
- Avoiding asking questions
- Saying yes to do things to avoid the discomfort of saying no
- Agreeing with others' opinions, even when one, in reality, *dis*agrees

Aggressive Behavior

When people become disappointed, irritated, annoyed, or angry, they may behave aggressively. Whether justified or not, their systems kick in with aggressive responses. Some people have shorter fuses than others and quickly react aggressively if things don't go their way. Other people react aggressively if they've been behaving *passively* for too long. They've acted nice and compliant on the outside—with the consequence that they've built resentment up on the inside. At some point, that resentment erupts in aggressive reactions.

Aggressive behaviors tend to be *personal* attacks instead of reasonably arguing the points of disagreement. That is *not* professional. It means that other people's ideas are not heard as they should be, and that solutions get dominated by people with aggressive behaviors. Or, that things get entirely out of control, and no sensible solution is produced at all. When people have habits of aggressiveness, it leads to personal conflicts or avoidant or fearful behaviors in other people, making collaboration suffer.

To be clear: it's acceptable to be appropriately *passionate* in dialogues with colleagues and business partners. People may feel strongly about things and have conflicting goals, resulting in intense arguments being exchanged. That's okay, as long as it happens civilly and professionally. The problem is when passion turns into aggression. Then it can turn ugly—and personal—and take the route of being destructive toward other people. That's why communication skills are so valuable. (We'll cover this in the next chapter.)

Some examples of aggressive behavior:

- Undue shouting or yelling
- Threats or intimidation
- Dominating the conversation so others cannot speak
- Invading other people's personal space
- Ridiculing and labeling others
- Using sarcasm to belittle others
- Using aggressive body language (e.g., rolling eyes)

Arrogant Behavior

When people behave arrogantly, they believe that they're more worthy, more important, or more intelligent than other people. They exhibit low tolerance and respect for others. They overvalue themselves and feel entitled to be seen as special and to have exclusive benefits. This stands in the way of expressing empathy, sensitivity, and gratitude toward others.

Most people immediately react negatively to arrogance. What, on the surface, may appear like strength is, in reality, a weakness—and it destroys respect and trust. The arrogant person risks being perceived as a jerk and may be avoided by others. Because arrogance and overconfidence tend to lead people to overvalue their own decision-making capabilities, it has led to many wrong decisions and disasters in business and politics. The history books are full of them.

So, while confidence is a strength and necessary, arrogance is a flaw. Confidence should never turn into arrogance. This is especially pertinent when people are very successful because they easily become *over*confident and step over the line into arrogance.

Some examples of arrogant behavior:

- Indicating to others to be superior
- A "know-it-all" attitude
- Arguing too much; wanting always to be right
- A "take it or leave it" attitude
- Feeling entitled to special treatment
- Disregarding other people's views without fair consideration, especially from people they consider less important or smart
- Running late; keeping other people waiting

Manipulative Behavior

When people behave manipulatively, they express their needs, wants, and feelings in indirect and masked ways instead of communicating them directly.

Manipulative behaviors take two forms. First, when people try to *get what they want* by manipulative means like misinformation or flattery, they are not being open and honest about their real motives. Second, when people try to *resist* or *avoid* doing something by manipulative or covert acts, they are not being open about their hostility, resistance, or anger.

People who behave manipulatively can be very frustrating to deal with for others, as their behaviors easily lead to conflicts and even permanent mistrust. Many know the feelings of hurt, confusion, and anger after having been manipulated. It's not easily forgotten.

Some examples of manipulative behavior:

- Spreading rumors or blame behind people's backs
- Being two-faced (saying one thing to your face, and another behind your back)
- Using insincere compliments, flattery, or charm to achieve something
- Deliberately working inefficiently

- Ignoring or giving people the silent treatment
- Telling white lies
- Withholding information that, in reality, ought to be shared

Negative Behavior

Negative behavior is criticizing, complaining, and being plain negative. Complaining and critiquing have their time and place, but if it's a habit of *excessively* seeing and commenting on the negative, that's a problem.

As a rule, openly complaining and criticizing should be about things you *yourself* can contribute to change. Things that are within your circle of control. For example, issues within a current project or task—that's where you can exert influence and constructively critique things. You may also be able to influence bigger matters, but the same rule still applies: if you want to voice your critique, you should be ready to also offer a solution or at least some constructive ideas. However, complaining just to complain (or showing how smart you are) isn't helping anything or anyone. Instead—as emotions are contagious—it may lead to a self-reinforcing (negative) loop with your colleagues. Negativity breeds more negativity.

Negative behavior is a major turnoff for most people who generally prefer a motivating and inspiring work environment. And nobody likes to be around excessive complaining and whining. Therefore, people who act this way risk being avoided or excluded.

Some examples of negative behavior:

- Criticizing or complaining without offering solutions or ideas
- Criticizing at a safe distance from face-to-face conversations
- Having a negative attitude toward customers or clients
- Ignoring the positive and paying attention to the negative
- Always taking the pessimistic outlook
- Being cynical
- Being chronically unenthusiastic

Professional Etiquette

Professional etiquette is rules that create a mutually respectful atmosphere and makes people comfortable around each other in the workplace. "Professional etiquette" might sound boring, but the effect isn't. As these behaviors are usually *expected*, it attracts negative attention if you seriously deviate from them.

The particular way that professional etiquette plays out differs between cultures and workplaces, but as rules-of-thumb, what's described here should be appropriate almost anywhere. You obviously also need to learn any *other* etiquette rules specific to your current organization. They may be quirky or illogical, but, in general, try to stick to your organization's culture and peculiarities, as changing them will be an uphill battle.

Be Polite

Be polite and use good old-fashioned manners like saying "please," "thank you," "you're welcome," "excuse me," and "I'm sorry," or whatever version of these fits in your culture. Use polite gestures every time; don't start skipping them just because you think "it isn't necessary" or you're "too busy." There's no downside to being courteous. Also, stand up if you're sitting when you meet someone or are being introduced.

Be on Time

Be on time or even a bit early. Being late sends a signal of arrogance or sloppiness if it happens repeatedly. Especially when attending meetings, it's important to be on time and not to keep other people waiting.

To be exact, being on time means *on the minute*, so to be on the safe side, it's best to calculate on being a couple of minutes early and to include any time you may need to get coffee or refreshments. If you have meetings scheduled back-to-back, the general rule is to leave the first meeting before it ends so you can be on time for the *start* of the next meeting (you usually want to notify the host of the first meeting that you'll leave a bit early and then quietly leave when you need to).

Being on time is nearly always possible if you prioritize it sufficiently because, essentially, it's a choice inside your circle of control. Anyway, *if* you get delayed by things outside of your control, inform those you're meeting as soon as you know that you'll be late and indicate by how much you expect to be late. For example, with a simple message like, "Sorry, I'm running ten minutes late."

Dress for Your Role

Since work is a social activity, the rule for personal appearance is to blend in with your pack—or, at least, not to stand out negatively. Other people have other expectations and biases and will interpret how you look through *their* lenses. So, basically, you'll want to avoid attracting negative attention by *conspicuously* under- or overdressing.

The determining factor is your organization's culture and, more specifically, your job role. So dress according to the expectations for your job role. You can probably get some hints by observing successful colleagues. And check if your organization has a dress code you're expected to follow. Note also that in most workplaces, your personal grooming and hygiene have to live up to some minimum standards; smells of sweat, dirty nails, oily hair, and so on are usually big no-nos.

Speak about Others as if They Were in the Room

This easy-to-remember rule is a great reminder to not bad-mouth or gossip about others behind their backs. It doesn't mean you can't disagree with others who are not part of a conversation. Instead, it means that you always express your opinions in ways that you would be willing to repeat to their face.

In the same way, let gossip and bad-mouthing stop with you. Don't pass it on. If someone hears you gossiping about someone else who is not present, how can they know that you wouldn't do the same to *them* behind their backs some other time? The bottom line is that gossiping and bad-mouthing others destroy trust. It's a behavior you don't want to take part in.

Don't Bad-Mouth Your Workplace or Group

When you're with people from outside your organization, it gives a confusing and unprofessional impression if you talk negatively about your workplace. Imagine you're at a conference, and someone starts attacking and criticizing their own organization. That's a perplexing experience: If it's so bad, why doesn't this person find another job? No, your organization provides you with your livelihood, so you should represent it respectfully to external parties, including what you share on social media. Of course, the exception to this rule is when you're with your trusted inner circle. That's where you can discuss your frustrations.

Handle Confidential Information with Care

When others share information with you in confidentiality, do not pass it on to anyone, however tempting that might be. Never break the trust of others. People never forget that. Confidential is confidential. And if you're in a job where you work with classified information, respect that some information is so secret that you cannot even share it with your partner; you share it with *nobody*.

When handling written confidential information, make sure you do not unintentionally share it with someone it was not meant for. Therefore, double-check the recipients before sending any confidential email—or, if printing, double-check that it's the right printer you're sending your print to. Don't leave confidential information lying around or discuss anything confidential in public (e.g., airplanes or hotel lobbies).

If you, for some reason, believe that what others have shared with you *really* needs to go further, ask their permission first. However, there is one (rare) exception to this rule: If you become aware of seriously wrong stuff going on—sexual harassment, fraud, theft—then it's your professional duty to bring it to the attention of the appropriate persons in your organization. It would be misplaced loyalty to keep confidentiality in such cases.

Don't Use Inappropriate Language

Don't use inappropriate language or suggestions with sexual insinuation toward anyone. Ever. This is work.

Don't Discuss Controversial Topics

Some topics are volatile and touchy. They easily lead to heated discussions that may end up making people feel resentment toward each other—quite unnecessarily, as these situations could have been avoided in the first place by not discussing the touchy topics. For example, politics, religion and beliefs, sex life, money, and personal finances. As conversation topics, they share the problem that people are often emotionally biased, so different opinions lead people to get agitated or feel offended. Even though *you* may be fine discussing controversial topics, you can safely assume that many others are *not*. So stay away from them unless you know people very, very well.

Minimize Office Distractions

Noise and distractions can be a big problem for all those who work in open-plan or cubicle-type office environments. The worst kind of distraction is generally other people's conversations because they are difficult to block out. Consequently, keeping one's voice down is really important. And if you need to have a conversation with someone that's more than just a short exchange, go somewhere else where you aren't disturbing others. Don't be the office jerk who loudly chats away, oblivious to the annoyance and distraction of others.

For the same reason, don't use loudspeakers when you need to listen to something. Use headphones. Have your phone on silent or low volume, and remember to take it with you if you leave your workplace.

Finally, *think* before you interrupt someone. It's often all too easy (and tempting) to impulsively ask questions or share something in an open office. But that can be very distracting if it happens too frequently. It's usually possible to batch some topics together and then make just *one* interruption, which is longer in duration. That goes a long way in cutting down interruptions.

Special Considerations for Working from Home

The hybrid work model—where people work some (or most) of their time from home—is a fact of modern work life. Some people will rarely—or never—physically meet their colleagues, business partners, or even their manager. They may have *seen* their faces in online meetings, but not actually *met* them. Does that change how you behave?

The answer is no. When working from home, the basic rule is that your behaviors and standards shouldn't differ from when you're at your workplace. If in doubt, ask yourself, "What would I do, and how would I behave, if I were at work?"

For example, your office hours should be, more or less, the same because that's the most convenient for your colleagues—you can all reach each other at the same time. If you want to deviate from that, first agree with your team and manager. Also, dress as if you were at work, especially if you might find yourself in a video call with a short warning.

Etiquette for Business Meals

Whenever you're out for lunch or dinner or taking part in company events like holiday parties, remember that you are still *at work*. Hopefully it's enjoyable, but it's still a more formal situation than with family and friends. Meals with customers or business partners are important settings where people from both sides can share a common experience—*and* do some business.

Business dining etiquette differs between cultures, so if you're with people from another culture and don't know their traditions, investigate the differences beforehand to avoid unintentionally insulting or embarrassing them. In any case, the below rules-of-thumb should work almost anywhere.

First, *professional behaviors don't change* just because you're at a restaurant or some other venue outside of work. You can relax a bit here and there, but you generally want to behave as professionally as when you're at work. That also means you need to be careful with your alcohol intake (if any). Getting drunk is generally a huge mistake.

Second, when *ordering* food and drinks, a good tip is to follow the lead of the host or someone senior to you. Then you'll get some cues about the price range from the menu you can choose from, whether or not to order a starter, dessert, or coffee, and whether or not to order alcohol. You can also get cues by asking what others plan to order or simply wait and see what they order.

Third, follow *table manners*. That's the norms for using utensils, glasses, and nap-kins; when to sit down and when to start eating; appropriate eating and drinking pace; whether or not you can leave food on your plate; when to leave the table, etc. If you don't know what is expected, you can come a long way by following your host's lead, observing what others are doing, and using common sense.

Fourth, when making *conversations*, try to find a good balance between busi-ness and casual conversation. Business meals are never 100 percent business; some socializing is part of the game. And usually, the expectation is to start with some socializing before getting into business. Note that some events are pure relationship-building, where no business discussions are expected or even desired. If in doubt, ask someone familiar with the event you're attending.

Finally, be respectful of the host by *not complaining* about the venue, the food, or the service—even if it's justified. Just ignore any mishaps with the food, the service, etc., and focus on having a good time together.

Formal Workplace Policies

In almost all organizations (except the very small), you will find formal workplace policies in policy manuals or handbooks. Sometimes very elaborate documents, they detail the organization's policies on a wide variety of areas, including working hours, breaks, holidays, sick time, overtime, training, travel and expenses, alcohol and drug use, grounds for termination, employee performance reviews, confidential information, employee dating, accidents, use of email, internet, social media, telephone, vehicles, and more.

These policies are important to know and understand, as they give you the formal guidelines for what you can and cannot do. Use them for everything they cover; they're there for a reason and have probably been developed and honed over many years—in some cases, to comply with laws and regulations. If you're in doubt about how to interpret or follow the policies, ask your manager.

In addition to the general policies, your particular job function usually also has formal processes and protocols, which could be timesheets that must be filled in, reports that have to be written, records that need to be updated, systems that must be kept up-to-date, and so on. While few people love to do these administrative tasks, the professional behavior is to *get it done* on time and without complaining. It has to be done, everybody knows it, and everybody has to do it—even if the procedures and systems are sometimes difficult, slow, outdated, or illogical.

SKILL 6

COMMUNICATION

- Make an effort to understand. If you don't understand, ask.

- Adapt your communication to the receiver.

- Nobody can read your mind. Speak up.

Since work requires people to actually work *together*, communication has enormous significance in making it effective and pleasant at the same time. Poor communication is the cause of all kinds of unnecessary problems, including conflicts, misunderstandings, lost opportunities, negativity, and mistrust. That's why excellent communication skills are so valuable.

Common Principles

Eight common principles are fundamental for all professional communication. While they sound simple, they're not always easy to follow. But as you practice—and maybe shed old habits—you will communicate more effectively.

Communicate as Required by Your Job

One of the difficult but essential characteristics of professional communication is deciding *when* to communicate. Some people behave too passively and communicate too little, too infrequently, while others communicate too much, too often. So getting it right is a *balance*. If you don't communicate enough, you'll leave others wondering what you're doing and what your plans are. People may also think you're not contributing as you should. On the other hand, if you communicate too much and share every thought in your head—or get overly domineering, insistent, or repetitive—you risk putting people off. So, in short, you should communicate as much and as often *as your job requires* and not be influenced by any desire to be liked, fear of embarrassment, personal agendas, etc.

Have a Genuine Desire to Understand

Communication often goes awry because the people involved don't even *try* to understand each other. They are so preoccupied with their own convictions that they don't have the capacity, or patience, to understand the other party's position. The human tendency to evaluate, judge, approve, or disprove what other people say gets in the way. And that's a recipe for lousy communication.

What counts is that you have a genuine desire to understand. Put yourself *in the other person's position*—be empathetic and try to see things from the other person's perspective. Let's say you're in sales and trying to sell your product to a reluctant customer. In that situation, it would be wrong to just push and push with arguments about your product's qualities. If you do that, you'll fail to understand your (potential) customer's situation. Instead, if you do your utmost to *understand* first, you might find that you should emphasize other parts of your offering, or determine that your product is not relevant to the customer and stop your sales effort.

Trying to understand doesn't mean, though, that you should automatically *agree* with the other party's viewpoints; understanding and agreeing are two entirely different things. In fact, the most productive results often come from *differing* points of view that are explored together in constructive dialogue. Oppositely, without a mutual desire to understand, you're stuck in a pattern of *debate* where each party is endlessly defending their own views without really wanting or trying to see things from the other side.

Adapt to the Style of the Receiver

We are all different and have our own distinctive, natural communication styles. So when you're communicating with others, think about how *their* styles differ from yours and try to adapt to that. For example, extroverted people tend to speak what they think *as* they think, whereas introverted people tend to think a few seconds before they talk. Some people prefer written communication, whereas others prefer meeting up or speaking by telephone. Some prefer a high-level overview first and the details afterward; others like it precisely the other way around.

Therefore, it's crucial to acknowledge these differences to enhance the communication. For instance, if someone is terrible with email but excellent when talking with others, then don't send endless emails. Instead, grab the phone or have a meeting in person. By adapting your style to that of those you communicate with, *you* are doing *your* best to ensure a productive dialogue. Of course, it's both parties' responsibility, but you should always be doing your part.

Speak Up

Organizations need people who assert themselves, especially when it's not the easiest or most popular message they deliver. They need people who serve the organization's best interest by communicating what they honestly believe, which may not always be what their colleagues, managers, or customers like to hear. But finding the courage to speak up may be just what is needed to change a locked situation or avoid a looming failure. Of course, speaking up might not always be appropriate for a specific time and place; in some cases, you may have to stay silent. But as a general communication principle, it's professional to be as open as you can within the limits of the situation.

Be Clear and Direct

Professional communication is as clear and direct as possible. You don't want to leave room for misinterpretation. You want to make your message sufficiently complete so the receiver can take definite action on it. It should be so clear that it cannot be misunderstood: the more concrete and less abstract, the better. For example, "We need more resources for our project" can be made concrete by adding how many resources, when they're needed, for how long, and what kind of resources. Like so: "We need one more developer for six weeks, starting November first." Then you don't leave anything to interpretation (or *mis*interpretation) by the receiver.

You also want to explain any abstract concepts or abbreviations you use. Don't assume that other people understand abstract or complex concepts the same way you do, or that they use the same abbreviations. Since people often don't ask for an explanation, you do them a favor by providing one anyway. Likewise, avoid unnecessarily complex or academic language that people in your organization won't understand, as this language is not needed or even desired. On the contrary, where the school system often encourages academic language, it's all about ease of understanding at work: make it as simple as possible for as many as possible to understand your message.

Be Brief

A few concise statements often communicate with more weight than a long explanation. However, as simple as it sounds, being *brief* is not necessarily the same as being *fast*: it requires time to structure your ideas and arguments concisely. Mark Twain formulated that paradox in a funny way as "I didn't have time to write a short letter, so I wrote a long one instead."

Even if you dislike being brief because that would mean you would have to drop some of your points, do it anyway. It's much worse not to get your main message through because it drowns in other, less important messages. And if people need more information or more details, they can always ask.

State Your Main Point at the Start

Whether in written or spoken language, communicate the message of primary interest to *the receiver* immediately at the start, then elaborate on the details and background *after* you've delivered your main message. That way, you don't risk the receiver getting distracted or impatient before you come to your main point. This order of presenting is opposite to what the school system often teaches: that you first introduce your topic, then go through your main argumentation, and finally come to a conclusion.

Note, though, that some situations and cultures may require a more careful approach, where the main point is only made after paving the way with an analysis to avoid misunderstandings and make it easier for people to accept the conclusion.

Make It Positive

In general, people collaborate better if their mutual communication has an overweight of positive content versus negative. The more you can communicate in a positive, appreciative manner, the more others will enjoy working with you. And that means that you sometimes need to make an effort to communicate as positively as you can, even if the main issue is by nature negative. For example, you can say to a colleague who you believe is making a mistake, "You can improve that by . . ." or "I believe there is a better way." That's more positive than saying, "That's the wrong way." In essence, you're saying the same thing, but you state the message more positively.

You can also make your communication more positive by simply *adding* positivity when it fits. For example, you can almost always find a way to start an email with a short statement of appreciation like, "Thank you for your quick reply" or "Thank you for taking time." If you think about it, you can nearly always find something you appreciate, even when your main message is negative.

Conversation or Writing?

Fundamentally, people communicate in two ways:

1. **In conversation**—be it in the same room, by telephone, or in video calls. This is also called *real-time* communication.

2. **In writing**—by email or in collaboration apps (here, the term *email* is used for both), via text messages, or via social media. This is also called *asynchronous* communication because people don't have to respond immediately but can wait until convenient.

What to choose—conversation or writing—depends on the type of communication you are having. Choose *conversation* when:

-   You need to build trust and grow your relationship with other people. The ability to read each other's tone of voice and body language facilitates a richer communication experience than written communication. It also allows a bit of off-topic social dialogue, which further strengthens the personal relationship.

-   The topic is sensitive or may get emotionally charged. It's easier to assess the other person's reaction and avoid misinterpretations or overreactions in conversations. This also applies to giving corrective feedback, which should be done in person.

-   The topic is complex, which usually makes it long to write. And it may be hard to understand without the option to have a dialogue. In any case, a long email has a risk of not being read *at all* because of its length.

-   You need to negotiate details. Negotiating details can, of course, be done in writing but is usually more effectively done in real-time dialogue.

-   You need to investigate or problem-solve something together. When you need to collaborate in-depth, real-time is most effective.

- You need to discuss something confidential and don't want to have the conversation documented—as it otherwise would be if it was in writing.

- Something is urgent, and you don't want to risk the time lag of asynchronous communication.

And choose writing when:

- The other person needs time to think things through. Sometimes people cannot give their best answer while thinking on their feet but need time to collect their thoughts and provide an adequate and structured reply.

- The other person is busy and cannot give you the attention you need, here and now.

- You need to communicate the same message to many people.

- You need to document the conversation and attachments.

- Your message is merely informational, one-way communication.

- You work in different time zones and cannot have a real-time conversation.

Use these guidelines—not your personal preferences—for choosing whether to have a real-time conversation or to write. Even if you're uncomfortable with conversations with people you don't know well, if it's the best choice for the type of communication, still do it. For example, sticking to writing when you really need to have a personal interaction is not professional; instead, pick up the phone or hold a meeting in person.

Conversations

When having conversations with other people, what's the best way to make them pleasant and productive? That question has been the topic of numerous books and training classes, as it's a critical skill. With the guidelines below, you'll be well on track.

Be Respectful of the Other Person's Time

When you both know how much time you have, it creates the most relaxed atmosphere. Agree with the other person how much time to spend on the conversation, and let him or her know when the time is nearly used up. For example, you can ask, "Do you have twenty minutes to discuss X?" and then, near the end, note that "now we have five minutes left, so let's wrap this up." *Always* end on or before time; that's professional use of the other person's time.

Use the same technique to also be respectful of *your own* time.

Give the Other Person Your Full Attention

Next, be sure to give the other person your full attention. If you're constantly distracted by phone calls, messages, or email checking—or generally unfocused—it makes your conversation partner feel insignificant and unvalued.

So give the other person your concentrated focus and put your phone away, your laptop to the side, etc. Get rid of anything that distracts you. Have the conversation as if you're speaking to a very important person or someone you really admire. Make the other person feel like the only person in the room. If you can't do that, it might be better to postpone the conversation until you can.

Be an Active Listener

Listening is (at least) half of what makes conversations productive. For instance, in high-stakes negotiations, active listening is key to finding solutions that benefit both parties. And regardless of the outcome, people always feel valued when they've been sincerely listened to.

Active listening is (obviously) not a passive activity. Indeed, it's a process where you're *actively* involved in understanding the other party by paraphrasing what they're saying, asking clarifying questions, and so on. Consequently, active listening implies that you discipline yourself to focus on *understanding* what the other person is saying, and *why* they are saying it. And if you miss or don't understand something, stop the other person and ask for clarification or repetition; that is *also* active and respectful listening.

However, if you're only waiting for your next chance to break in and state your opinion or give your advice, you aren't really listening. Instead, that hinders your ability to focus on what the other person is saying.

Moderate How Long You Talk

Next—and in line with the principle "be brief"—you want to moderate how long you talk before the other part can come into the conversation. Lengthy statements or monologues don't work because people will not remember everything you say if you speak incessantly for minutes on end. And people are likely to get impatient or annoyed. So don't be so eager to present your case—or make a good impression—that you speak too much and take charge too often. On the contrary, good conversations give space for *both* people to talk and extend on each other's ideas. Consider if it's even worth saying what you have on your mind; sometimes, it's prudent to pause for a second and contemplate, "Is this really needed?" The best action may be no action.

Manage Interruptions

If you get interrupted (which is usually unavoidable), there are several ways to handle it. Provided that the interruption is unjustified and you don't want to be interrupted, you should simply demand to continue, in a polite and neutral tone, without sounding offended or irritated. For example, say, "Please let me finish," "Hear me out," "Excuse me, I wasn't finished," or other variations. People often don't realize they have interrupted you and will let you continue and even apologize. Another strategy is to simply raise your voice a bit and continue, ignoring the interruption. Or you can just wait until the other person has finished speaking and then resume what you were saying.

Of course, in general, *you* shouldn't interrupt others. It can offend people. However, there are exceptions: if someone has misunderstood something and is now going entirely in the wrong direction. Then you can politely interrupt by saying, "Sorry, I believe you misunderstood" or the like. You should also interrupt if someone is unwittingly monopolizing the conversation by rambling on about something or gets caught up in their own enthusiasm. Then you can respectfully say: "I'm sorry to interrupt, but . . ."

Actively Use Your Body Language

Your body language also matters in conversations. A lot, actually. In fact, it's so important that it can be a determining factor in job interviews. Much of what you communicate is not in your words but in your eyes, stance, and gestures, and whether you're smiling or nodding. Consequently, it's not only what you say that counts; it's *the whole perception* the other person gets of you: words *and* body language. You cannot *not* communicate with your body language; it's always telling something.

First, eye contact is critical. The appropriate amount of eye contact differs between cultures, and it's important to live up to those expectations. In Western cultures, eye contact shows that you're engaged and attentive—it's a sign of respect. And avoiding eye contact can be interpreted as being nervous, uncomfortable, uninterested, dishonest, or plain rude—not exactly what you want to communicate.

Second, your posture speaks. For instance, sitting or standing erect and confident signals that you are open, positive, and relaxed and can also help you *feel* that way. In contrast, if you assume a slouching position, slump your shoulders, or make yourself small, it signals that you're uninterested, tense, or insecure. But that's only half of it: in addition to being mindful of your *own* body language, try to observe your conversation partner's body language. That can give you some great nonverbal cues to how comfortable, confident, enthusiastic, or anxious he or she is.

Third, smile and nod in your conversations when you want to signal positivity, interest, and agreement. That adds an extra dimension to the conversation. In contrast, if you *fail* to smile or nod, your conversation partner may interpret it that you're not interested or misunderstanding.

Email

Written communication skills are often as critical as conversation skills. Written communication (often email) is an immensely effective tool, but if used inappropriately, it confuses people, wastes time, and lessens the sender's credibility.

Because many people are overwhelmed by the volume of emails, the key strategy is to communicate clearly while minimizing the time spent by *everyone* (not only you, but all the receivers of your emails). The following practices will help you get it right.

Make Emails *Short*

Being brief and to the point may be the difference between an email being read or "saved for later when I have more time" (which often is *never*). A crisp email of a few sentences has a higher likelihood of being read, not to mention *understood*, than an email that fills the screen. And that's important, as people often have to speed-read their emails. Imagine that you only have a half hour between meetings, and you have twenty-seven new emails in your inbox you need to process (a realistic scenario in some jobs). Then you definitely need to speed-read!

So the more concise you can make your emails without sacrificing clarity, the better. As emails are often read by many people, the time you save by writing a short email can be multiplied by the number of recipients. Thus, a brief email may save *hours* of reading time for the whole organization. That also means that you shouldn't state the obvious or write things people already know. Instead, stick to the core message and don't waste the recipient's time. Consider these two examples:

- "Unfortunately, we cannot rearrange our priorities, so the earliest delivery date we can make is May 5."

- "As we discussed during the last couple of months, it would probably be challenging to change our plans to come up with an early delivery date. In our team, we have been discussing various rearrangements of our priorities and several alternative solutions. Still, we have not been able to come closer to what you are looking for. If you wish to discuss this further, I am, of course, more than willing to do so. But, as it stands, we will not be able to make the delivery before May 5."

Admittedly, this example is slightly exaggerated, but unfortunately, such unnecessary wordiness is common. Even if the short version may seem terse, remember that people can always ask if they need *more* information.

Structure Emails for Easy Reading

In line with the principle "state your main point from the start," make sure that your main message, or any specific action the receiver is supposed to take, is stated right from the beginning. The only exception is if you want to make a short, positive or appreciative sentence first. But otherwise, friendly or rapport-building sentences should go at the end.

If you want an answer to a question, ask a direct question that conspicuously stands out by giving it its own line or italicizing, boldfacing, or underlining it. That way, the receiver cannot be in doubt about what you're looking for. For example, put a question like, "*Will three working days be enough to finish the contract?*" in italics. The same goes if you have an important deadline, want to emphasize urgency, etc.

You also want to make your email as easy to read as possible, so use paragraphs generously; they make your email look easier to read. And use bullet points to add clarity when applicable.

Choose an Appropriate Writing Style

Be mindful of your writing style; an *informal* style may be right in some situations, just as a *formal* style may be required in others. But be cautious with the informal style: your email may be forwarded. Sometimes a seemingly insignificant email—written *very* informally—may suddenly grow into a string of emails forwarded to recipients you never imagined (for example, a customer or someone in top management).

Only use exclamation points (!) and all caps letters (LIKE SO) sparingly; a style with runaway exclamation points and unnecessarily capitalized words is easily interpreted as aggressive and unprofessional. Be cautious with abbreviations and acronyms; not everyone knows FOMO, IMHO, or your profession's technical abbreviations and acronyms. So it's best to avoid them or only use them when you're sure that all perceivable recipients know them.

Finally, be *very* careful if you're angry or annoyed. Your bad mood is likely to shine through in your writing style and result in an email that you'll later regret. Remember that emails live forever! So, if you write an email to someone you're mad at, don't send it impulsively, but let it cool off in the draft folder for a few hours or until the next day. Then reread and edit it before sending, or get a colleague to review it before you send it.

Choose a Concise Subject Line

After writing the main body of your email, write a subject line that's a shortened version of the main message and action statements. The subject line is essential because it's the main hook that tells the receiver what the message is about. It can make all the difference in whether or not people even open an email. It's also important because when people search in their old emails, it's easier to find the right one if it has a descriptive subject line. Consider starting with "For information" or "Action required," as this helps the receiver understand the purpose of the email. Make it as informative as possible: "For Info: Updated Parts List, Product #1234" or "Action Required: Review Q1 Report before Tomorrow, Noon."

Proofread

When you're finished writing, proofread your email for correctness, clarity, spelling errors, and punctuation errors. Pay attention to facts like dates, names, numbers, amounts, product codes, etc.—they *must* be correct.

Another tip is to read important emails aloud to help you find logical errors and improve clarity and readability. Or ask a colleague to proofread it.

Choose Only *Needed* Recipients

People are often overwhelmed by the number of emails they receive because they get so many that they don't need. Therefore, every time you compose or reply to an email, contemplate if your message really *is* necessary and helpful for all the recipients. If not, you might as well remove them and save them the time. As well, be careful with unconsidered use of the "Reply All" feature—many people just continue to "Reply All" on a long email thread, leading to a lot of unnecessary emails flying around. Instead, stop and *think* if all the recipients on the list really need to receive the email.

And don't put anyone on copy (Cc:) if they have an action to make. Copy (Cc:) is only used to *inform* people, not when they should *do* something.

Respond Timely

So, how quickly should you respond to emails? First, that (obviously) depends on the urgency of the matter. Some emails need a response almost immediately or within hours. And others can wait for days without that being inappropriate. It also depends on the sender's expectation; some people have higher expectations than others. For example, managers, important customers, or people who generally work under time pressure may expect quick responses. In any case, *putting off* replying to emails and just letting them sit in your inbox is clearly unprofessional—don't do that.

If you know you're unable to make a timely and satisfactory response, let the sender know *when* you can reply. That's more professional than letting the sender wait with *no* information from you. For example, you can reply, "I'm busy with X, so I'll not be able to review Y before Monday." Then the sender knows what's going on. If you're away at a conference or workshop, or traveling, then use the out-of-office function to notify people about what response times they can expect from you and what they should do if they urgently need to contact you. For example, that they can send you a text message.

Meetings

Depending on your job, meetings can take up a significant part of your time. And while many meetings are necessary and productive, others can be time wasters. So, to minimize time spent in meetings, try to:

- Only hold the necessary *meetings.*
- Only invite the necessary *attendees.*
- Only spend the necessary *time.*

As obvious as this sounds, these principles are unfortunately often broken: unnecessary meetings are called, with attendees not needed, consuming more time than necessary. And nobody likes to see their time wasted. So the main goal with meetings is to make them as productive as possible for everybody. The following are some good practices for *attending* meetings.

Different Types of Meetings

The first step in making meetings productive is understanding what *type* of meeting it is. Four fundamentally different types of meetings are:

1. ***Information* meetings,** where the purpose is to communicate information or messages, often to many people simultaneously. This is typically in the form of presentations of upcoming changes, new products or services, or in-depth domain knowledge—maybe with an option to take some questions. But they are *not* for discussing things,

and they should end as soon as the information is communicated or the set question time is over.

2.   *Problem-solving* **meetings,** where people put their heads together to creatively solve a problem, generate ideas, think up new solutions, or make plans. This type of meeting is where people discuss things in-depth and are creative together. These meetings work best with a limited number of attendees, preferably no more than ten, and ideally three to seven.

3.   *Status* **update meetings,** where everybody in a group updates each other about what they're working on, their progress, what challenges they have, and what they do to address them. This is everybody-to-everybody information sharing to align a team so that everybody knows what's going on. The idea is to mutually exchange information; therefore, these meetings should not derail into spontaneous problem-solving meetings.

4.   *Team-building* **meetings,** where the purpose is to create a feeling of cohesion and togetherness in a group. There may be little or even no work content whatsoever—the idea is to build relationships within the team and have a good time together as a group.

The critical point is to know what type of meeting you're in at any given time—and then stick to that. The different types of meetings have different purposes that shouldn't be mixed. Otherwise, they quickly stop being effective and erode into time waste instead. For example, during a status update, no attendees should start a discussion to solve someone's issues. Instead, they should agree to have *another* meeting, where only the relevant people attend, to work on the problems.

However, note that some (longer) meetings *combine* agenda points that are each a different meeting type. For instance, an agenda may consist of a status update session, someone presenting a matter in-depth, and some working sessions to problem-solve current topics. That's typical with team meetings. So when you're in one of these meetings, be aware when you switch to a new agenda point; it might also be a change of meeting type.

Accepting and Declining Meetings

The next step is to accept and decline the right meetings. When you get a meeting invite, respond to it promptly to help the organizer plan the meeting; they need to know who's coming and who's not. And keep your calendar up-to-date so that organizers don't waste their time inviting you to meetings that you, in reality, cannot attend.

However, don't automatically accept *all* meetings; your time is too valuable. If you're not sure if you're the best person for the meeting's topic or if your attendance is really required, it's appropriate to ask the organizer to clarify the meeting's objective and your role in it before accepting. If you then believe that your presence is not required and that you could spend your time more productively, it's okay to decline it. That's not rude or uncooperative but rather demonstrates responsibility.

When you decline, do it politely and cooperatively. For example, if you believe that a colleague is better qualified for the meeting's topic than you, suggest that the organizer invite him or her instead of you. You can also offer another way to contribute your input, such as in writing before the meeting.

Attending Meetings

When attending meetings, follow some best practices to make them as productive (and least time-consuming) as possible.

First, know what *role* you have in the meeting; depending on the type of meeting, you may need to review some material in advance or prepare something. Or you may need to have conversations with others. Whatever is required, it's essential to come well prepared so you don't waste everybody's time because you, for example, did not read a document that all the other attendees read.

Second, stay focused on the business at hand when you're in a meeting. Be actively engaged and *don't* check or respond to emails or text messages; you cannot effectively be engaged in a meeting while working on other things on the side. Think about how *you* would like it if you were presenting and many of the participants were texting or emailing and clearly not paying attention. If you (exceptionally) have to work on something on the side, then inform the host and the other participants what you're doing and why. For example: "I'm sorry, but I have to check my email from time to time, as I'm expecting X that needs my immediate approval."

Third, be mindful of the agenda and the time allocated to each topic. Help the host make the meeting effective by doing *your* part to ensure that you and everybody else stay on topic and on time. This is not only the host's responsibility but something all attendees should participate in. Before you speak, consider if what you have to say is really relevant for the meeting. Many meetings take longer than necessary because people see them as opportunities to talk (sometimes at painful length) about topics that are irrelevant to the issues at hand, or they waste time repeating what someone else said, but just in their own words instead of a quick "I agree." Don't be that person. Instead, it's professional to only speak when one has something substantial and relevant to contribute—and then speak concisely and with impact.

Meeting Minutes

If you take the meeting minutes, either write them during the meeting or right after. If you wait too long, you'll not only forget a lot about what happened but you will also spend more time making them. The art of writing meeting minutes is to make them as concise as possible while still holding all the relevant information. Most often, only the actions and decisions agreed in the meeting should go into the minutes, *not* the discussions that took place (unless explicitly asked for). If in doubt, ask the meeting organizer. Remember to include all the basic elements:

1. The meeting's name, place, date, and time
2. A list of the participants, including those who were invited but didn't attend
3. The agenda
4. For each item: who is responsible for what, when
5. The date and place of the next meeting, if applicable
6. Any documentation (e.g., presentations, reports, etc.)

If you didn't capture a decision, conclusion, date, name, etc., ask for it to be repeated during the meeting so you get it correct.

Virtual (Online) Meetings

In virtual meetings (with or without video), follow the best practices outlined previously, including joining the meeting a few minutes early. If you follow those practices, there are only a few differences to online meetings:

- When you join, and if it's not otherwise visible or apparent, announce yourself. It's awkward when you hear the sound indicating that someone just joined, and it's followed by . . . eh . . . silence.

- If you join late, never ask everybody to introduce themselves. It has probably already been done by the time you managed to join.

- If there's background noise where you are, put yourself on mute when you're not speaking.

- If there is no video transmission, say your name before you start talking, unless you're sure that everyone on the call recognizes your voice.

- If there are several people in the same room on a voice call and others are sitting alone, the people in the room should be aware that those sitting alone cannot see what is going on in the room. Therefore, they should explain what's happening in the room. For example, if people are nodding or shaking their heads, drawing on a whiteboard, entering or leaving the room, etc. Also remember to ask for the opinion of those who are not in the room.

Preparing for High-Stakes Situations

When facing high-stakes situations—like a critical meeting or presentation, a difficult one-on-one conversation, a challenging negotiation, or a job interview—*prepare* well to give yourself the best odds of a successful outcome.

As obvious as this sounds, *lack* of preparation for high-stakes situations is common; many people try to just improvise and hope for the best. But that's a lousy strategy—and unprofessional. Preparing well is key to raising your confidence and obtaining a good outcome. For example, preparation for a high-stakes meeting of just one hour may take *weeks* if there's a lot at stake.

As part of the preparation, try to *anticipate* the questions and objections you might get. Think them through beforehand, and don't naively assume that you won't get them. You may even want to *write down* the questions and objections you might encounter—and your answers. That also has a calming effect, as you now know how you'll handle the most difficult situations you anticipate. For example, if you're preparing for a performance review meeting with your manager, you can write down the challenging questions and feedback he or she might have for you—and your answers. Those answers are also easier to remember when you have calmly thought them through *before* the meeting.

You can also rehearse. Let's say that you're preparing for an important customer presentation. Then you'll benefit from simply practicing it out loud. By doing that, you can hear any incoherent argumentation and get a better sense of the timing. Another option is *role-playing*: enlist a colleague to play the role of a skeptical customer who has objections to what you present. Then switch roles so you also get to play the role of the customer.

Tricky Communication Situations

Some communication situations are notoriously tricky or awkward to handle. Those situations call for specific strategies. We have picked six common situations with suggestions for how to manage them. All the preceding communication practices still apply; these strategies are the *extra* things you can do.

Communicating with Angry and Unreasonable People

When people are angry and unreasonable, their communication skills and ability to view things from the other side are severely reduced. Therefore, the best strategy is to postpone the conversation with the angry person to another time when he or she has cooled down. As that can take several hours, it may be best to suggest that the conversation is postponed to the next day.

However, postponing is not always possible. For example, it may be unfeasible if you're dealing with customers, patients, clients, etc. So if you cannot post-pone, how do you handle the angry person? The best place to begin is with the principle of "Have a genuine desire to understand." Listen actively and *genu-inely* try to understand the reasons behind the angry person's frustration. That, by itself, is likely to have a soothing effect on the other person's mood—and *you* may better understand the situation. You may also find that there are valid reasons for the other person's anger and that *you* have done something that triggered it. In that case, apologize and move on with the conversation from this new starting point.

If you cannot postpone the conversation, and trying to understand doesn't work, you should stand your ground. You have *your* opinion, and you'll not change it regardless of how angry the other person is. The best way to do that is to *repeat* your point of view until you're heard. For example, if someone is angry with you because you haven't time to do something, you can repeatedly assert yourself: "Sorry, but I don't have time to do that" . . . "Sorry, but I don't have time to do that" until the other person gets it. The key is to have a simple message that *you don't divert from*—and repeat it until you're understood.

If nothing else works, you can choose to walk away, maybe proposing that you talk the next day instead.

Communicating with Bullying, Rude, or Abusive People

Much different from people who are *temporarily* angry, some people have (unprofessional) bad *habits* of being bullying, rude, discriminating, intim-idating, or abusive toward others. If they start displaying their bad habits toward you, you should nip the behavior in the bud the *first time* you meet it. Immediately address their behavior to prevent it from taking hold—don't be passive and accept it. Instead, make eye contact, take a confident posture, and assert yourself straightforwardly:

- "I find that statement offensive."
- "Please stop that."
- "There is no need for that tone."

With clear statements like this, most people will back off: this is *work*, and their behavior is unprofessional. Remember that *their* behavior is *their* bad habit, not something you should take personally. You cannot change the person (that's outside your circle of control), but you can do your best not to let their behaviors affect you (which is inside your circle of control).

If their bad behaviors toward you persist—despite your sincere efforts to stop them—you should consult with your manager about the situation.

Communicating with Passive People

Even though passive behavior is unprofessional, you should still make an effort to involve passive people; they may just have low confidence and otherwise be fully capable. Try to make them feel comfortable so they can contribute without feeling under pressure.

The best way to do that is to encourage them to contribute by actively asking for their points of view, actively involving them in team discussions, and being an active listener. Also, use your body language to emphasize your encouragement by nodding, smiling, keeping eye contact, leaning forward, and so on. Finally, hold back in conversations and group discussions to give them space to express themselves.

Giving Feedback

Where Skill 1: Self-Awareness addressed how to *receive* feedback, this skill is about how to *give* feedback. And everybody needs to give feedback, not just managers. For example, you may be instructing a colleague, a customer, or a client and thus, you may need to correct and advise them.

Remember that you shouldn't hold back giving feedback just because you want to avoid hurting the recipient's feelings. Giving corrective feedback is *respectful* because it shows that you *expect* good performance from the recipient and believe they can do it. Oppositely, if you *don't* offer feedback for faulty performance, you're indirectly communicating that you have low expectations and rob them of the feedback they actually need.

When giving feedback, do it as soon as possible. Don't sit on it "for later"—that risks being *never*. The best time is often right at the moment when you are *in* the situation. If the feedback contains an element of criticism, give it when both of you are relaxed; neither can be angry. And in most cases, don't do it when others are present.

With that said, follow these three guidelines:

1. **Be direct.** It's best to just be straightforward; feedback is feedback. You don't have to be subtle or indirect or apologetic.

2. **Be specific.** The more specific, the better. You want to address the *actions* or *behaviors*, not the person. So don't exaggerate, and don't be vague; be precise. For example, don't say, "Your presentations are confusing." How would that help? Instead, you could say, "This morning, when you presented the results from the customer survey, for me, it would have been a clearer message if you had started with the results first. I suggest that next time . . ." That's specific.

3. **Make it useful.** Focus on *changes* that the recipient can make. It's easy to criticize, but not necessarily so easy to devise solutions. Therefore, helping the recipient comprehend how to do something *right* is more important than what went *wrong*. Useful feedback is something that the recipient can do something about. For example, "You should always calibrate the scales before using them to ensure they're weighing correctly" is much more helpful than "You're not using the scales correctly."

Giving Compliments

When someone is doing something you admire or appreciate, tell them! If you don't, they won't know that you're thinking these positive thoughts. Use these three guidelines to give great compliments:

1. **Be sincere.** Compliments should come from the heart—they should be honestly meant. Don't give compliments that could be misinterpreted as shallow or coming with an expectation of getting something in return. Instead, give compliments when you *feel* admiration, *feel* enlightened, *feel* elevated—then they will come out as sincere and believable. Just straightforwardly say what your spontaneous reaction was. It isn't complicated, so don't make it.

2. **Be specific.** As with feedback, be *specific* and detailed about what you liked; then the receiver knows what to do more of. Think about what exactly it is you appreciate about what the other person is doing. For example, "I like how you presented the results first before drilling down into all the explanations—that made it very clear." That's much better (and more useful) than "I really liked your presentation." It also makes your positive feedback more credible, as it shows that you were paying attention.

3. **Ask questions.** Optionally, you can supplement your compliment by asking questions. That's another way you can demonstrate your genuine interest. You express not only your praise but also add a question or two to elaborate. Continuing on the previous example, you could follow up by asking, "How did they react to it?"

Apologizing

If you make a mistake or say or do something that hurts others, you need to apologize. A good apology motivates people to let go of the past and move forward. Here are some tips for how to apologize.

First, the worst thing you can do is *not* to apologize at all. It's one thing to do something that hurts others, but something entirely different not to admit it! *Not* apologizing is *also* communicating something and can cause more ill will and damage to your relationships than the original offense you made. So don't be too defensive, proud, or vain to admit that you were wrong: offer an apology when you need to. Don't rationalize or minimize your responsibility—apologizing is not a sign of weakness. Quite the opposite: it's a sign of self-worth and generosity.

Next, apologizing isn't difficult. Start by acknowledging what you did and don't excuse, explain, or evade it. If the other person wants to talk more about what happened and how that affected him or her, listen actively without being defensive. Then apologize by saying "I'm sorry" or "I'm sorry that X." It shouldn't be complicated or include any element of "but . . ." where you start to explain yourself; that just devalues the apology. It has to be unconditional and sincere. You may also want to add your intention to not do it again: "I'll try to do better" or "I'll not do that again." The key is to not make it long or complicated.

Finally, if you can make amends or help fix whatever problems your actions have created, then do that.

SKILL 7

TEAMWORK

- Focus on "we," not "me."

- Trust is earned.

- Don't make disagreements personal.

Most things at work are done in collaboration with other people; very few people work entirely independently. Because you often cannot choose *whom* you work with—your colleagues, your managers, your external partners—you'll have to work with them despite any differences in skills, values, worldviews, and personalities. Consequently, teamwork skills are necessary.

Your team also has an enormous influence on your job satisfaction and happiness. If you're in a good team where you feel trusted, respected, and valued, it's a deeply satisfying experience. It will enable you to create exceptional results together that none of you could have done on your own. Even if your organization isn't necessarily a great place to work, it can still be a great place for *you* if your *team* is great. Oppositely, if you're in a dysfunctional team, it doesn't matter how great your organization is; *you* will likely feel lousy and want to get out of there. So your *team* is your home; that's where you, first and foremost, have to function well.

Note that cultures and school systems differ when it comes to teamwork: some put a lot of weight on collective achievement; others focus more on individualism. Because of these differences, the behaviors described in the following will be more natural and familiar to those brought up with teamwork and collective achievement.

In Teams, People Complement Each Other

The idea of a team is that its members complement each other, with each individual having a specific role and contributing their unique skills and natural strengths. That way, the weaknesses of each team member don't count much. Instead, it's the *best* of everyone that's brought together to form a strong team. Everyone does not have to be good at everything; that would go against the organization's purpose, which is to bring skilled individuals together to create something that no one can accomplish alone. Like components in a machine, each team member contributes *their* individual skill set.

For example, a team that sells IT projects may consist of an extroverted and outgoing salesperson, a product specialist who designs the offerings, and an industry specialist who knows the customers' typical business problems. Each of them will have different strengths, weaknesses, values, and interests, but together, they *complement* each other to form a strong team. And no one in the team has to be good at everything, and no one expects it. Each team member can be happy with their own role and be equally happy that they don't have to do any of the other roles.

For you as a team member, this idea of the team means three things:

1. **You must be good at the role *you* are hired to play in your team.** To make the team perform, *you* must play *your* part. For example, if you're employed as a product specialist, you must do your best to be competent in that role. That's where you should focus your effort;

think, "What is *my* responsibility?" On the other hand, you can be less worried about your weaknesses, as they are (hopefully) covered by the others in your team. And if you struggle in your primary role, you have to do something to fix it—for example, by working with your manager to upgrade your skills.

2. **You should respect the other team members' roles.** Know which role *you* have and know which roles *they* have. Think, "What are my teammates' responsibilities?" Don't cross the boundaries of your teammates' roles and start doing their jobs or take control of their domains. Unless, of course, you explicitly agree that you should do that. The product specialist shouldn't begin to play salesman—and vice versa.

3. **You should think, "Where does *the team* need *me*?"** Sometimes some tasks and responsibilities don't fit naturally with any one team member. When that happens, the appropriate team behavior is to offer to contribute with what's missing, provided that you have sufficient skills. How can *you* additionally contribute to the team's needs? You're not in a strong team if people evade and make excuses when something has to get done.

Focus on "We," Not "Me"

It's not your production as an *individual* that—in the end—counts; it's the production of the *whole team*. It's the team's results that matter: If the team wins, everybody wins. And oppositely, if the team loses, everybody loses.

What does this mean for you? It means that you should think first about your team's common purpose and put your personal agendas second to that. Your own desire to get recognized or develop your career (or whatever goal you might have) shouldn't be leading what you say or what you do. When you talk—*in* your team or *about* your team—talk about "us" and "we" more than "I" and "me." Paradoxically, talking about "us" and "we" will make you shine more in the eyes of others and make you sound more confident than if you talk about yourself first.

Additionally, focusing on the common purpose means that:

- You spend time together in your team to coordinate your work, confirm that everybody understands the shared goals, ensure nobody is doing redundant or unnecessary work, and make sure nobody is sitting idle. Everybody needs to know what *they* should work on and how that fits into the team's puzzle. Even though this coordination sometimes doesn't feel like "real" work, it's essential to ensure that the *team* works effectively and to avoid having a few individuals work well at the expense of the team's effectiveness.

- You do whatever work is needed in the team and (unselfishly) contribute as best as you can. That may sometimes mean jumping outside of your job description to work on something that you're overqualified for or weren't educated to do. Or it could mean helping someone reach a deadline or supporting someone who lacks a certain ability. And sometimes it means working some extra hours to reach a goal. However, it should never mean that you work so much that you burn out due to your loyalty to your team.

- You freely share skills, knowledge, and experience that may benefit your teammates. To the extent it can help others be more effective, you share documents, knowledge, practices, templates, and methods— you don't keep them as private assets. And you don't wait for others to *ask* you; you offer what you have voluntarily and unsolicitedly when you can see that it can assist others. In the same way, you can ask others for *their* best assets to make your work better and quicker. Of course, some people with an individualistic mindset may resist, but don't let that hold you back. In any case, when you act first and take the initiative to share, people are also more likely to follow your lead another time.

- You give credit to the team when things go right and take accountability when things go wrong. When you have successes, you share the praise and recognize everyone involved. You don't try to take the credit yourself, as that's unfair and selfish and your colleagues will resent it. Even worse, don't take credit for the work of others; that's almost like stealing (and it sure feels like it). Oppositely, when things go wrong, you take accountability and avoid blaming others; be honest about it if you have contributed to a problem or a failure. When things go wrong in your team, the best you can do is to learn from the experience and channel it into improvement—*together*, as a team.

- You celebrate together when your team is successful. When you've reached an important goal or milestone, you don't just let it pass but make sure to celebrate it together and enjoy the achievement. That's fueling the team spirit with new energy.

Build Trust

Trust is the key building block in teams, if not in all human relationships. When people trust each other, they can put their guards down, risk being vulnerable, and put their full effort into their work. They can test each other's ideas and afford to disagree. On the other hand, if a team *lacks* trust, people will spend valuable time protecting themselves; they won't share their ideas, mistakes, or skill deficiencies as much. And they won't ask for help. Lack of trust makes a team much less effective.

Importantly, trust is *earned*; you don't build trust by just talking about it. Instead, trust is created when people *work* together. Specifically, trust is built via four behaviors that complement each other: being sincere, being reliable, being authentic, and forgiving others. Each of these behaviors contributes to people trusting each other. The more you exhibit them, the more people will trust you.

Be Sincere

The base of trust is that other people perceive you as sincere, a person of integrity, a person they can take seriously. That's the foundation, and it means several things.

First, sincerity begins from within, with being honest with *yourself*. That you *mean what you say*. Let's say that a colleague asks you to do something, and you answer, "Sure, I'll do it today," even though you know deep down that you'll probably not have time to do it until tomorrow. Then you're saying something that you yourself don't even believe. You're merely expressing an *intention* to do it "today." But the other person will perceive it as a commitment. The acid test is what you would have done *if no one was watching*. In this example, you would not commit yourself to "today" since you doubt it yourself.

Being sincere also means that you tell the truth as you honestly believe it to be. That you *say what you mean*. If a colleague comes up with an idea that you believe is unworkable, you can straightforwardly say why you think it is unworkable (in a respectful manner, of course). Or if your manager asks you for your opinion, you answer honestly, even if it's not the answer he or she would most like to hear.

Additionally, what you *say* and what you *do* needs to be the same thing—you want to "walk the talk." Your *actions* should speak louder than your words. If you talk to others about the importance of being on time but then are late yourself, you come across as a hypocrite.

For people to perceive you as sincere, you also want to be *consistent* with every-one. If people change their opinions depending on who they speak with, they don't seem trustworthy. Thus, being consistent means saying the *same* thing to everyone, regardless of who they are. It also means that you don't cut corners with your own standards; you don't allow yourself to deviate "just this once." That's not being consistent.

Finally, you want to be *accurate* with what you tell others. People quickly lose trust if you present things to them as *facts* that are, in reality, rumors, gossip, guesses, or wishful thinking. Instead, you should only express facts that you're sure of. If you're not sure, qualify your statement: "I'm not sure about this, but I believe that . . ." Trying to sound more confident than there is evidence for just detracts from your trustworthiness.

Be Reliable

Another aspect of trust is that you are reliable, that people can depend on you to *keep your promises*. Let's say that you're a carpenter and commit to showing up at a customer's address Wednesday morning and the customer makes special arrangements to stay at home that morning to meet you. Then you'd better be there, or the trust is gone.

The key to reliability is to make an effort to deliver what you promised, when you promised. And to keep your promises, you must, in the first place, *be diligent with what you promise*. Don't make a commitment unless you honestly believe you can keep it. Instead, be as accurate as you can and err on the side of *not overcommitting* if you're in doubt. That also makes it easier for your colleagues to work with you when *their* plans depend on *your* commitments. The same goes for making forecasts and estimates, like sales, cost, resources, time, production, etc. Here you also want to be as accurate as possible and not inflate or deflate your numbers to look good or for political reasons.

Similarly, you want to *clarify* expectations before you commit to doing something. You don't want to commit to doing anything *un*clear. People often make unclear requests, though they may be clear in their own heads. If you don't ask for clarification, the requester will probably assume that you understood it the way he or she meant it to be understood. So if you're in doubt, make sure to clarify things before committing.

If something happens (out of your control) so you cannot keep a promise after all, then inform others who need to know as quickly as possible. That's the professional way of handling expectations when something slips—you don't just wait and hope for the best. It preserves as much trust as possible even in situations where you cannot live up to expectations.

Be Authentic

Being authentic means that you are *you*—and not putting up a show to impress others or to live up to what you believe others (might) think. Most people have a well-developed sense of detecting when others are trying to appear brighter, faster, more competent, or more successful than they really are. When they perceive others as fake or pretentious, they immediately find them less trustworthy.

The tendency to conceal one's weaknesses, failings, and skill deficiencies is human. But to build trust, it's better to *allow oneself to be vulnerable*, to be straightforward with both one's strengths *and* weaknesses. Basically, to be accurate about one's competence and neither overstate nor underrate it. That gives a balanced presentation of who you are. Because trust is more important than being seen as a bit smarter or more confident than you really are. You know it better than anyone if you're not being true to yourself, so if you find yourself with this feeling, stop for a moment and ask yourself what you're doing and why, and adjust your behavior if you need to.

So, to build trust, you need to shed your need to be *in*vulnerable and engage in behaviors that help you be perceived as authentic. The following team behaviors will do exactly that:

- Admit it when there's something you don't understand, don't know, or are not sure about. Don't pretend to know or understand when you don't. Admit it and ask clarifying questions, ask for repetition, or ask for a more detailed explanation.

- Accept suggestions, feedback, and questions from others about your work. Don't be defensive. You don't have to *agree*, but you need to respectfully listen to advice and input that others wish to give you.

- Accept it when your teammates hold you accountable. If you're not living up to what you committed to or if you behaved unprofessionally, it's only correct and helpful that other team members tell you so. Don't make excuses or blame others when something really *is* your responsibility—that only makes you look worse and lowers others' trust in you.

- Ask for help. Everybody needs help and guidance (not least at the beginning of their careers). So don't be too embarrassed or afraid of being rejected to ask for help. Your teammates will probably be more helpful than you think. Asking for help is a natural and necessary team behavior, so don't feel like you're a nuisance when you do it—you're not.

- Actively ask others to offer differing opinions and to test and challenge your arguments. *Seek* opposition to check if your ideas and arguments are valid and can stand the test of others scrutinizing them.

- When you make a mistake, straightforwardly admit it and take responsibility for it. Without undue delay, communicate to those who need to know that you've made a mistake. That way, you can fix it when it's still small and manageable. If you wait, the consequences will often be worse. And don't (over-) explain or (over-) excuse your mistake if it *is* indeed yours. Even worse, don't try to *conceal* a mistake, as people will immediately lose trust in you when you're found out.

- If you break someone's trust or make a mistake with negative consequences for others, quickly apologize to restore their trust in you. Giving people the opportunity to forgive you is a way to regain their trust.

Forgive Others

Sometimes people do things that impact you negatively. They make mistakes, behave disrespectfully, are inconsiderate, or make decisions that don't go your way. Or, in a heated moment, they say things they shouldn't have. While it's natural to get upset when these things happen, it's unprofessional to fume with resentment for too long. You want to let go of those feelings sooner rather than later. Being negative, resentful, or even vengeful destroys trust. Therefore, you have to come to terms with what happened and *forgive*. Let it go. That's the professional attitude. Then you can move on, and 1) not let the negative feelings drag you down and 2) get on with rebuilding the relationship. Of course, it's not everything other people do that you can forgive, and that's okay—sometimes you'll come across people with ill intentions whose behaviors cannot easily be forgiven. But most situations at work *can* be forgiven.

You may also want to take the initiative to clear the air and let the other person know that you don't hold grudges. Doing so can only earn you respect. By wiping the slate clean, you and the other person get a new chance to regain trust and work productively together. That may be as simple as saying, "No hard feelings," or something more serious where you meet and talk the situation over. What's important is that you take the initiative to fix the issue between you.

Manage Disagreement Constructively

Disagreement and conflicting interests are part of the design of organizations: different parts of the organization have opposing needs, and resources are scarce.

For example, a natural conflict often exists between sales and production in a commercial organization. Sales will typically want *more* product variants to get more sales, while production typically wants *fewer* variants to reduce production costs. Conflicts like this are inherent in how the organization works, so the employees *must* find solutions that satisfy the interests of both parties. The conflict is impersonal: the conflicting views are part of the job descriptions, and the conflict is productive—one that has to be constructively resolved regardless of which individuals hold each job position. Therefore, making such conflicts personal is meaningless. Since the conflicting goals come with the job roles, the cause of the conflict is not other *persons,* but the way work is *organized.*

This is a crucial dynamic to be aware of, as these differences in roles and needs can escalate to "us-versus-them" conflicts, where teams or even whole departments are nagging and bad-mouthing each other. If you experience this, take a step back and consider if the other people aren't just doing their jobs. Try to see things from *their* position and understand what *their* needs are—before you judge! They are, in all likelihood, not trying to make your job difficult, but simply doing what is sound logic from *their* perspective.

Disagreement and conflict are also natural and unavoidable between people with different *personalities.* That may be between detail-oriented people and visionaries, or between introverted and extroverted people. Neither of them is wrong, and they should respectfully work together to make their differing personality traits complement each other, despite their natural disagreements. They should appreciate each other's differences and see them as complementary to themselves instead of strange or wrong.

A third example of natural disagreement is when people have different *values*. Recall the work values described in Skill 2: Setting Goals: 1) money, security, and status, 2) social connection, and 3) self-expression. Such differences in values often lead to distinctly different views on the same issues and situations. Again, professional behavior is not to let the different values lead to conflicts but to understand them for what they are and as complementary to each other.

So, as disagreement and conflicting interests are natural and unavoidable, how do you make the most of this "constructive tension"? The answer is to simultaneously do two things: 1) engage in the disagreements that are part of your job (don't avoid them) and 2) maintain trust and stay on topic (don't make it personal). Let's go into detail with each of these essential team behaviors.

Engage in the Disagreements That Are Part of Your Job

To work effectively, people need to be candid and straightforward with each other. They need to openly share their opinions and acknowledge disagreements and problems. If they don't, they'll miss out on valuable input and issues will remain unresolved. Remember that the *common purpose* should drive anyone's actions—even if they risk awkward moments or interpersonal discomfort by calling out problems and disagreements. That's why being (respectfully) candid is so important: it makes *the team* more effective.

So, before anything else, it's essential to *engage* in the disagreements that are part of your job—don't withdraw from or avoid them. Professional behavior is to take the conflicts and address the problems and disagreements that necessarily have to be resolved. Avoiding the necessary disagreements, issues, and conflicts is like avoiding your *job*. And the kind of "harmony" you gain by avoiding is fake and forced because the conflicts still exist. They just change character and instead become latent tensions that people can still feel anyway.

Maintain Trust and Stay on Topic

Few people ever get completely comfortable with conflict and disagreement. Many are—at least to some degree—conflict-averse.

That's why it's important to *maintain trust*: it creates an environment where people can feel safe to speak up about sensitive and conflictual topics. When people trust each other, they can feel safe to be vulnerable, take risks, disagree, and passionately discuss things. With the right—trusting—environment, having disagreements and conflicting interests doesn't need to be uncomfortable. Because with trust, it's okay to have disagreements as long as everybody is constructively trying to produce solutions that support the common purpose. And if the common purpose is hard to see, the parties can *zoom out* far enough to get a perspective that covers both of their interests. For example, sales and production can easily see that they need each other: without sales, there will be no orders to produce, and without production, there will be no products to sell.

In addition to maintaining trust, it's crucial to *stay on topic*. That means to stay focused on the business at hand and on objective data, information, observation, and analysis instead of getting personal. By staying focused on the business at hand, there is less risk that someone gets personal and regresses into unprofessional behaviors. Arguing with personal statements like, "Oh, you are so X . . ." is strongly unprofessional.

But what do you do if you want to *say what you mean* but also want to *avoid upsetting* others? What do you do if you worry that you'll hurt or make people angry if you're sincere? How do you solve this dilemma? The answer is that it doesn't need to be a dilemma at all. You can have both. But you need to communicate carefully so that neither of you gets personal, angry, or defensive. The key to keeping disagreements constructive is to stay focused on two critical principles:

1. maintain trust
2. stay on topic

As long as you can do that, you're on the right track.

However, what do you do if these two principles start to break down? That can be separated into two cases: Whether 1) *you* or 2) *the other person* loses trust or gets off topic.

First, if *you* lose trust in the other person, *you* need to slow down. The initial signs that you've lost trust will be changes in your mood or behavior. Therefore, you need to monitor yourself for such changes that indicate you've lost trust. For example, are you getting defensive, sarcastic, or aggressive? Are you getting passive and silent? Are you holding back relevant information? Are you exaggerating? Do you get personal and attack the other person? Do you change your arguments to save face? Or jump to conclusions or start mind reading the other person?

If you recognize these emotions and behaviors in yourself, interpret them as cues to step back, to *not* act. Ask yourself: "Have any automatic thoughts taken control of my behavior?" Remind yourself that you have the freedom to *choose* another behavior and that your automatic thoughts are *just thoughts* rather than something you *must* react to. If you feel that you're getting angry, you can ask for a time-out: "Please, let's take a step back to why we're here" or "Let's stop this discussion for a moment; I need to roll back to X." You can reset the conversation and zoom out to the broader perspective with statements like those. That gives you a chance to dig yourself out of a conversation that has gone awry.

Second, if *the other person* loses trust or goes off topic, you need to reestablish trust and bring things back on track. The signs that others are uncomfortable and losing trust are the same as when *you* lose trust. For example, they get passive and silent, or (at the other end of the spectrum) upset, aggressive, or personal. When that happens, don't let yourself be provoked by this behavior, but interpret it as cues that the other person feels uncomfortable, unsafe, or vulnerable, or that they feel their rights have been violated.

Whatever the reason, you need to try to bring the conversation back to a place where the other person feels comfortable. And the remedy is the same as if it were you: zoom out to the broader perspective and your common purpose. You can suggest, "Let's set aside this discussion for a moment, and X."

Also, if *you* have indeed contributed to trust being lost, you should do *your* part in restoring it by using the trust-building behaviors mentioned previously. For example, by apologizing or taking responsibility for your mistakes.

Commit to Jointly Made Decisions

Teams often find themselves in situations where they *have to* make a decision but cannot find a solution that *everybody* agrees to. There is, simply, disagreement about what the right decision is. But still, a decision *has* to be made, and the team members must commit and be loyal to the jointly made decision.

As obvious as this sounds, it doesn't always happen that way; people frequently fail to follow the team decisions *they* disagree with. They (stubbornly) go their own ways, despite a group decision they were a part of. And that's destructive to the team's effectiveness—and the team spirit. The principle to fix this is called "disagree and commit":

1. Everybody has the right to be heard and the right to *dis*agree. Notably, everybody must *speak up* if they disagree—they cannot simply sit back and passively resist what's happening. If something is important to them, they must put their opinion forward. In short, the first part of the principle is that you stand up for what you believe in.

2. When the team has made a decision, everybody must *commit* to it, whether they are in favor of it or not. Thus, the second part of the principle is to be loyal to your team's decision, even when you would have preferred a different one. Loyally implement what the team has decided and don't complain, be bitter, resist, or undermine the decision.

Hold Each Other Accountable

In a team, people need to hold each other accountable when they fail to do what they committed to, make mistakes (and don't notice themselves), are unresponsive, don't respect deadlines, or deliver lower performance than agreed. Holding others accountable is not just the job of managers; instead, in effective teams, people hold *each other* accountable. That's also *respectful* because it shows that you expect good performance from your teammates, that they live up to their commitments.

While this sounds easy, people often find it uncomfortable to do. Many would rather tolerate a colleague's inferior performance than face the discomfort of holding him or her accountable. They fear that their relationship could be affected; they fear that others may react negatively with defensiveness or anger. Or embarrassment or guilt. All feelings that we don't want to induce in others. That's why it's tempting to avoid or procrastinate holding others accountable.

However, *not* holding others accountable is not in the *team's* best interest. It severely weakens the team's effectiveness if delays, substandard performance, or running from commitments become normal and acceptable. More than that, team members may start lowering their *own* standards just because others are doing it: "If *they* don't do it, then *I* don't have to do it!" That's a downward spiral, which starts when people begin to avoid holding each other accountable.

But then, *how* do you hold others accountable? First, don't delay it; that just makes it more awkward and may escalate the consequences. Then, it isn't much different from giving feedback: you want to—respectfully—be *straightforward* and *specific* about the problem: "Jimena, please comply with the document standard we all agreed to. I noticed that X . . ." or "Frank, the deadline for your input was yesterday, but I haven't received it yet. I really need it now. Can you please send it today?" These examples are straightforward and to the point while also being respectful.

Note also that when you follow up on people, you shouldn't chase them in multiple communication channels at the same time. For example, you don't want to simultaneously send them chats, text messages, and emails about the same topic. That's over the top. It's better to pick a channel and wait for the answer in that one channel. Then, when you've waited a reasonable amount of time, you can follow up—but still in that same channel. You should only reach out in multiple channels if something is genuinely urgent and warrants an immediate response.

SKILL 8

WORKING WITH YOUR MANAGER

- Understand what's important for your manager.
- Be guided by your common purpose.
- Frequently align expectations.

The most important person for your job satisfaction and career opportunities is, very often, your manager. With the right manager—and the right relationship—you can have great opportunities for development and job satisfaction. Oppositely, if you don't have your manager's support, it can be difficult to thrive and be successful. And if you have antipathy and opposition between you, it will definitely be uphill. Thus, your relationship with your manager is critical. It's worth doing your very best to make it work.

Managers (like everybody else) come in all shapes and sizes and can have very different management styles; what is good practice with one may irritate another. Here are some (simplistic) descriptions of typical manager archetypes:

- **Authoritarian:** This type is strong-willed and direct and prefers to be in charge and talk and lead (and others to listen and follow). They like to make quick decisions and are not afraid of taking risks. They are highly results-driven—often toward short-term goals. And they may apply pressure to reach those goals.

- **Social:** This type prefers to lead by selling a vision, inspiring and involving others, and being informal and friendly with their teams. They value enthusiasm and creativity—often more than procedures, systems, and details.

- **Supportive:** This type is collaborative and leads by guiding and developing their teams. They highly value trust, sincerity, and helpfulness. They prefer stability, consistency, and gradual development toward long-term goals—not rapid changes and risk-taking.

- **Analytical:** This type is rational, conscientious, and task-oriented. They lead by a systematic approach, wanting to have clear guidelines and procedures for everyone. They are more formal and detail-oriented than the other types. And—often perfectionists themselves—they expect high-quality work from everyone in their teams.

Even if your manager seems very different from you—clearly having other skills, values, or personality—don't assume that your relationship cannot be positive. It can, if you acknowledge the differences. But you need to understand what's important for your manager and adjust your way of working and interacting accordingly. Treat every manager you have individually—like the individuals they are. *Not* modifying your way of working to your manager's style will typically result in misunderstandings and loss of trust and, over time, a deteriorating relationship.

Note that cultures differ significantly with regard to how you interact with your manager. This book takes the perspective of a Western culture, which differs markedly from Eastern or Middle Eastern cultures. So if you come from a Western culture and start working in another culture, you need to adjust. And vice versa, if you come from an Eastern culture and start working in a Western culture, you likewise need to adjust. Consequently, do some research on what the norms and expectations are in *your* workplace—for example, regarding hierarchy, respect for title, age, sex, decision-making processes, etc.

A clear example of cultural differences is when it comes to challenging your manager: in modern Western organizations (this book's viewpoint), it's *expected* that employees challenge their managers when needed, whereas, in others, it may be seen as *disrespectful* (and, therefore, needs to be done with the utmost tactfulness).

An Inside Look at a Manager's Job

You will never meet a manager who is *perfect*. Everybody has their own style, qualities, and shortcomings. You can consider your manager a special team member with extended authority but also a team member who, like anyone else, needs to be complemented by the rest of the team. So the best way to view your manager (and other managers) is as another human being with both strengths and weaknesses.

Importantly, managers have *two* roles:

1. to *manage* their teams and get results
2. to *be a team member* in their manager's team

The first role is all about creating results through the team the manager is responsible for. In this role, the manager will align each team member's targets and prioritize and reprioritize things along the way to reach the team's overall targets. To do that, the manager needs a capable team that can deliver. Consequently, the most important part of this role is supporting and developing the individual team members to be effective in *their* jobs. If someone on the team is not performing or negatively affecting other team members' performance, it's the manager's responsibility to do something about it. The manager is also responsible for staying within budget, or getting approval to go above it. That goes for salary increases, training, tools, expenses, materials, supplies, telephone—anything and everything that costs money. It all has to be within the budget, which puts clear restrictions on the manager's opportunities for action.

In the second role, the manager is *a member of* his or her manager's team. In this role, the manager is an *employee*, just like you, who has to deliver agreed-upon results to his or her manager. For example, if a manager's manager has to cut costs, this target will trickle down to all the managers in his or her team. This role is also much less autonomous than you might think because there is pressure from both up and down: this double role requires balancing between the needs of the team and the needs of the manager's manager. On top of that, there are processes, policies, constraints, and dependencies to always be taken into consideration.

Keep in mind these two roles your manager handles. That will often make it easier to see things from your manager's perspective and understand the decisions made.

How to Interact with Your Manager

So, how do you actually interact with your manager in your daily job? These four principles can always be your guide:

1. **Be guided by your common purpose.** Like in your team, the driver of your relationship with your manager is your *common purpose*. You and your manager revolve around your common purpose, but you don't revolve around your manager. This principle is fundamental for understanding the nature of your relationship: you should not see yourself as dependent on your manager but, rather, see the two of you as dependent on each other as parts of a larger system. Both you and your manager should be guided by the needs of those that your organization ultimately exists to serve: customers, patients, citizens, students, clients, and so on.

2. **View your relationship as a partnership.** Your relationship with your manager is not a one-way relationship; instead, you should view it more like a partnership. Although the two of you are not equals in

terms of power position, your manager *needs* you; consequently, you *also* have power in the relationship. Your power comes from your skills, knowledge, natural strengths, and track record of successful accomplishments. And it's best if your relationship is in balance where both of you mutually contribute to each other's success. That means, on the one hand, that you don't want to be too submissive or pleasing—and, on the other hand, that you're not too much in opposition or too demanding. Even though your manager has the ultimate responsibility, you *frame* your relationship in a more balanced way by viewing it as a partnership.

3. **Deliver your part.** In a partnership, there are two partners. One of them is you, and to be a valuable partner, you need to deliver *your* part. Performing as you're expected to is the most critical factor in making your relationship with your manager a partnership. If you're not producing the expected results, it will be difficult to enjoy much of a partnership with your manager. Similarly, you (of course) expect your manager to deliver his or her part: support, development, respect, and your salary.

4. **It is okay to disagree with your manager.** When needed, you can disagree with—and question—your manager. Because the two of you are in it together, driven by your common purpose. Like with other team members, you need to engage in the disagreements that are part of your job. That only makes your manager more effective because he or she isn't always right and needs to be challenged like everyone else. Obviously, your ability to disagree with your manager is limited when you're new in your job. But as you gain competence and confidence and build your track record, you *earn the right* to disagree and question. The better you become, the more weight your opinions have, which gives you the authority to disagree on those occasions where it's needed.

These four principles are the foundation to build a good working relationship with your manager. Based on them, there are some specific behaviors that you should follow. We're covering them next.

First, Get the Basics Right

When it comes to your manager, you want to make an *extra* effort to follow the professional and team behaviors and communicate right (as described in the previous chapters). From your manager's point of view, if you cannot follow simple etiquette rules, come late for meetings, are negative or manipulative, don't communicate clearly, and so on, you are far away from being perceived as a partner. On the other hand, if you're on top of these skills, you're already well on your way to a good working relationship with your manager. So, get the basics right first.

Be Honest

Mistrust is a certain killer of the relationship between any manager and his or her team members. Without trust, the odds of creating a fruitful partnership are bad. And trust quickly breaks down if your manager starts suspecting that you aren't fully honest.

So you need to be honest with your manager. For example, when you cannot make your deadline or your numbers, don't hide it or postpone saying it. Or, if there's something you don't know or don't understand, say so. If you're asked about something you don't know, you can reply, "I don't know. But I'm happy to check it out." Or, conversely, if there's something you *do* know or believe you *can* do, say that and don't hold back. The key is to be *accurate*: what you say is what your manager will actually experience from you. When asked your opinion, answer honestly—*also* when you disagree with your manager's view. Don't hide or evade anything; trust is more important than hiding a mistake (and your manager may find out anyway). And if you know that some of your colleagues disagree with you, you must fairly represent *their* opinions, even when they differ from yours. You shouldn't try to shine at the expense of your colleagues.

Obviously, being honest with your manager can feel risky and may indeed be. Being honest is not risk-free, but neither is being silent or evasive because those behaviors diminish trust. Basically, building trust with your manager is never entirely risk-free, as it requires your honesty. But take a look at those colleagues who are closest to your manager (or other managers): they are usually the ones who dare to disagree and question their manager's opinions. They are typically listened to because good managers know they don't have all the answers themselves and need people who will challenge them and who they can openly discuss ideas and problems with. Good managers aren't afraid of surrounding themselves with people who are strong in their weak areas or are smarter than themselves. However, if people just tell their managers that they're right even when they're wrong or make mistakes, it's lack of critical thinking and goes against the common purpose. Good managers understand the difficulty and courage it takes to go against them—and they welcome it. But remember that the right to challenge is *earned*; you probably don't want to do it before you've gained adequate experience within your work area and have shown some solid results.

Being honest with your manager doesn't mean, though, that you should tell your manager absolutely *everything*. Especially, you don't want to run to your manager with every detail of what your colleagues are doing, what their opinions are, or what mistakes they're making. It's not your job to do that. Don't bad-mouth or gossip about your colleagues to your manager. However, if you're asked directly, you should answer honestly; you shouldn't cover up for your colleagues.

Focus Your Relationship on *Work*

To build trust, you need to shine through your *work*—not through *managing the impression* you make. That means that you should focus on the work you do with your manager and let your relationship build from that. Focus on delivering *your* part, on doing your *job*. Indeed, that's the only way your relationship can develop; it cannot be forced or willed into being. A good relationship grows through shared experiences from which you can build genuine mutual appreciation and trust. If you engage in flattery or strategic maneuvering to improve your image, you're on the wrong track. That's not how partners should work. Real partners work on creating results together to achieve their common purpose. They don't try to impress each other with empty acts, and they're not driven by personal (and hidden) agendas.

You also shouldn't try to make friends with your manager. You can, obviously, have fun together and socialize together, as you can with the rest of your team. But deliberately trying to be your manager's friend is misjudged. Focus your relationship on work and on your partnership. You may, indeed, share personal stories and emotions—as you do with every other colleague when appropriate. But don't cross the line into perceived friendship—keep it professional. For instance, don't invite your manager home to chill with you, or expect him or her to treat you differently from other employees because you think you are "friends."

Align with Your Manager before Anyone Else

Your manager needs to know what you're doing and what you're planning to do next.

When you have competing priorities, you should align with your manager. Often, multiple colleagues, customers, or patients want you to help them or do something for them, and you may come into a situation where you don't know what to prioritize. When that happens, align with your manager early and before anyone else: that prioritization is your *manager's* responsibility. And anyway, your manager should have a better view of the big picture than you. If you prioritize yourself, you could be wrong and start working on something that, in reality, isn't the highest priority. Even when someone pushes you, you should still (politely) reply that you want to align with your manager first.

Let's say you get involved in a project where it's initially agreed that you can spend one day per week on it. But your tasks quickly grow, and you now spend two days a week on it. In such a case, you must align with your manager to determine if that's okay and discuss which other activities consequently need to be prioritized down.

Bring Solutions, Not (Only) Problems

When you have a problem, you should try to develop some possible solutions before presenting it to your manager. You don't want to go to your manager with *only a problem* and ask, "What can I do about it?" Instead, you should also present some options for *solving* the problem, usually including a recommendation. That's taking responsibility for what's inside your circle of control. Which is, at least, to develop some ideas to address the situation and be ready to explain the pros and cons as you see them. That's what is expected from a partner, even if your suggestions may not be the final solution.

Resolve Internal Disagreements without Involving Your Manager

Sometimes, you'll have personal or professional disagreements with colleagues. In such situations it can be tempting to go to your manager and ask him or her to solve the situation or make a decision. But beware, it's usually better to first make a sincere attempt at solving the issue directly between you and your colleague. Often, when people go to their manager with internal disagreements, it's because they want to avoid the discomfort of managing the situation directly with their colleague. It seems easier and less uncomfortable to have their manager resolve it. But that's a poor excuse if it's something that you should, in reality, be able to handle between yourselves. So try to find the courage to solve it yourself.

However, if a sincere attempt doesn't solve the situation, you can (and typically should) go to your manager. Besides, your manager *needs* to know if conflicts, bullying, or unethical behaviors are happening on a regular basis, so that's another reason to inform him or her.

Don't Bad-Mouth Your Manager

Your manager has weaknesses and will make mistakes and wrong decisions at times. But that doesn't make it legitimate to bad-mouth him or her or engage in behind-the-back complaining or criticizing. You are both on the same team, so just like you wouldn't appreciate it if your manager started bad-mouthing and undermining you, the same goes the other way around. Team members should be loyal *both* when things go up *and* when they go down.

Likewise, if your coworkers complain about and undermine your manager behind his or her back, don't participate in it.

What You Discuss with Your Manager Is, By Default, Confidential

What your manager shares with you—comments, opinions, news, decisions, etc.—is, by default, confidential. For instance, you cannot run back to your team and entertain them with what your manager just told you. Unless, of course, you're directly asked to do so. Otherwise, you can of course ask for permission: "Is it okay if I share this with Anna?"

Did Your Manager Hire or Inherit You?

Note that it can make a difference if your manager is also the person who hired you. The person who hired you obviously wants to show that the decision to hire you was correct—and is usually extra committed to your success. And that starts your relationship on a positive note.

On the other hand, if your manager has inherited you from another manager, you will have to make a new beginning with your new manager. You cannot assume that you can continue to behave and communicate the way you did with your previous manager—that could prove to be a very wrong assumption (remember how much the manager archetypes differ.) So when you get a new manager, pay extra attention and make an extra effort to get your relationship off to a good start.

How to Communicate with Your Manager

The number one rule of communicating with your manager is to actually *do it*! Many are too modest or too timid to communicate enough with their manager. Or they believe their manager is too busy or too important to speak with them. However, that's a big blunder; frequent communication *is* necessary to build a good relationship with your manager.

But how often and how much should you communicate with your manager? That's a delicate balance because, on the one hand, you *do* need access to your manager to do your job, but, on the other hand, you don't want to waste your manager's time.

Meetings with your manager are often called "one-on-one" meetings and can be held in person or as audio or video calls. As a rule of thumb, it's productive and appropriate to have a conversation alone with your manager once per week. Or, as a minimum, every two weeks. If you talk less frequently—for example, once per month—you're not communicating enough and you're unlikely to create the kind of partnership you both need. That said, you don't necessarily need to spend more than fifteen or thirty minutes (and rarely more than an hour); what matters is that you *have* the interaction. Even if you don't have a particularly good relationship with your manager, it's still essential to have these one-on-one meetings—if not *more* essential.

To make it worthwhile and valuable for you and your manager, follow these guidelines for your one-on-one meetings:

- Always be well prepared.

- Relax, and don't be overly formal.

- Focus on your most important and valuable topics. It's far better to have a few topics thoroughly discussed than to bring so many topics that you have to rush through them. Be flexible if your manager wants to go in another direction than you planned.

- Agree on your priorities for the period until your next meeting.

- Ask for feedback.

- Take notes of anything you should remember.

You also want to observe the communication principle "adapt to the style of the receiver." You want to find the mix of written and spoken communication that fits your manager's habits and preferences. If you're unsure, it's appropriate to ask your manager what his or her preferred style is. Also, be aware of your *own* communication deficiencies. For example, if you know that you sometimes talk too much or get too technical, try to keep those tendencies in check.

Note also that asking for feedback is *especially important* with your manager—if you don't ask, you'll probably get less than you need. Many managers aren't any better than anyone else in that regard; they find it difficult or uncomfortable to give feedback, even though it's their job. So, if you don't get enough feedback, you have to ask for it. When you ask, use the techniques explained in Skill 1: Building Self-Awareness.

Besides your one-on-one meetings, you'll also need to have ad hoc conversations with your manager when things pop up that can't wait. Then—like with any other colleague—you want to be sensitive with your timing. Don't just burst into your manager's office and start talking when he or she is obviously swamped with work and trying to meet a deadline. Try to learn your manager's habits and rhythms: When is he or she most accessible and relaxed? Or, if something is urgent, simply ask for a short meeting: "Kirsten, I need fifteen minutes sometime today to X. When is good for you?"

Keep Your Manager Informed

Your manager needs to be on top of what's going on in the team. Therefore, you have to keep your manager informed about everything relevant—both the good *and* the bad news. It's annoying and embarrassing for your manager to learn about a critical issue from someone else because you didn't inform him or her first. No manager likes to be surprised or seem uninformed about things they really *should* know. So you need to keep your manager up to date on how things are progressing.

For example, if you run into problems, cannot meet a deadline, or cannot make the numbers you're expected to, you should inform your manager as soon as you think there may be a problem. Don't procrastinate. This is all about being proactive so you can involve your manager in a timely way in the issues you face—and your manager can take appropriate action or guide you in how to manage your issues.

Likewise, when things are going according to plan, or better or faster, you obviously want to keep your manager updated.

Useful Techniques When You Disagree with Your Manager

Sometimes you disagree with your manager. Maybe you have different opinions about something, or you're asked to do something you disagree with, or your manager makes a decision you disagree with. How do you then communicate your concerns?

First—and in line with the principle "it is okay to disagree with your manager"—you need to voice your concerns in the first place. When you do it, keep in mind that *you*, of course, could be wrong or could have misinterpreted something or have less information than your manager. So you want to be tactful and tread carefully, not the least because some managers don't take it lightly to be challenged (even when it's justified). And, as mentioned earlier, beware of cultural differences: maybe disagreeing with your manager is welcomed, and maybe not. For example, if social hierarchy, reputation, and "saving face" are important elements of the culture, you need to carefully consider this when sharing your disagreement; in some situations, it may be better not to share your disagreement at all.

The best approach is to discuss disagreements with your manager in conversation; don't do it in writing. Call for a meeting *alone* with your manager and make it informal and not tense. And, as with disagreements in your team, the key is to manage them without making them *personal*. You can, for sure, just be straightforward with your disagreement, but if you want to go easier, you can frame it to be less personal. For example, you can use one of these techniques:

- Frame the disagreement as if it's *you* who has a problem with something you're being asked to do or a decision your manager has made. You can say, "I feel uncomfortable dealing with twenty percent more clients without extra resources." When you frame your concern that way, you are not saying that *your manager's* decision is wrong but rather that *you* feel uneasy about it.

- Frame the disagreement in terms of your *common purpose* and your *team's* success. You can say, "I'm concerned that it will lead to lower quality and us losing clients," which can also be used in combination with the above technique. That way, you also link your concerns to your manager's success.

- Frame the disagreement as *questions*. By asking questions, you help your manager see the issue from other perspectives—hopefully leading to a dialogue about alternatives. You can ask, "What are some alternative ways of doing this?" or "Is there anyone who has another view on this?" or "What if those assumptions don't hold?"

- Frame the disagreement as questions *others* might ask. That way, you help your manager zoom out to see the issue from other people's perspectives. You can ask, "How would Mary respond to that?" or "What other alternatives might Kim want us to evaluate?"

- Frame the disagreement as something your manager can *think about*. Sometimes people simply need time to think things through, especially if it's a bit more complex. If they feel pressured to answer straight away, their only option might be to dismiss an idea or make a quick decision that's not well thought out. However, if you ask your manager to "think about it" and don't demand an immediate response, he or she gets time to reflect. So you want to plant some seeds for your manager to consider. Then you can take your topic up later when your manager has had time to think. You can say, "I would really appreciate it if you could come up with another alternative rather than giving me twenty percent more clients."

If you disagree with your manager *in public* (for example, in a meeting), be sensitive with your timing. First, consider if you actually *do* have to disagree in public or *if* the issue is better suited for when you can be alone with your manager. And if you disagree in public, then do it once, not repeatedly. If your manager turns you down—and you want to persist—then take the next round of dialogue in private.

Of course, disagreements with your manager will sometimes end up with your manager insisting on his or her standpoint (it could also be a top-down decision that your manager cannot change). In that situation, the principle "disagree and commit" applies: you have voiced your opinion and have, hopefully, been listened to and taken seriously. But if your manager won't change his or her opinion or decision, you have to do what you're asked to do; after all, it's your manager's *responsibility*. And it's *your* job to implement the decision with your best efforts, even if you don't agree. Don't undermine your manager's decision by giving it a halfhearted implementation that indirectly could make it fail.

In rare instances, a disagreement with your manager can be so serious that you may consider taking the issue with your manager's manager. For example, it could be a patient safety issue. But reserve that action for rare and severe situations—it's usually a better option to keep pushing your direct manager rather than bypassing him or her and escalate to a higher management level. And *if* you do it, don't do it covertly; rather, inform your manager that you will bring your disagreement to the next management level. And always consult with others before taking such a step, as it could be *you* who is overreacting or overinterpreting things, so you want to double-check for that first.

How to Align Expectations with Your Manager

You need to know your manager's expectations of you; you don't want to be uncertain about what you aim to accomplish in your work. As well, you want to *influence* those expectations. It doesn't have to be a one-way process.

The best way to align goals and expectations is to have *regular* interactions with your manager, where you check up on how you're doing. Preferably weekly, as previously discussed. If you rarely discuss goals and expectations with your manager (for example, only once per year), it's a recipe for *missing* the target. You cannot read your manager's thoughts.

If you don't feel sufficiently clear about what's expected of you, you have to be proactive. When appropriate, a good option is to take the initiative to include a checkup of your goals in your one-on-one conversations. Because you cannot live up to expectations if you don't know what is expected of you. You have to take the initiative to clarify it. If you're in doubt, it's better to find the courage to have the conversation than to live with the uncertainty.

Make Your Results Noticed by Your Manager

Aligning with your manager requires that he or she actually knows what you are doing. If your manager has incomplete information about how you work and the results you make, you risk that he or she will believe that you do less than you actually do, that your results aren't as good as they really are, or that you're not developing professionally. And you cannot count on your colleagues to report that you do well—they may, and they may not. Consequently, making your results noticed is something you have to do yourself. Somehow you have to be visible.

So, how do you get your good results across to your manager without it sounding like self-promotion? The best method is simply to work closely enough together to let the facts tell the story. If you work closely with your manager or at least have frequent one-on-one meetings, your manager should have a fairly accurate idea of how you're doing.

However, if you have less frequent communication and don't work together often, you need to do more. One way or another, you need to make sure that your manager knows what you're doing and what your results are. One option is to send your manager a weekly update on what you've been working on, your plans for next week, and any major issues you're facing. In line with good communication practices, make it brief and to the point: just the facts, nothing wordy, and not the details. Just something that's easy and quick to consume in a few minutes. Think of your update as *helpful*—remember, your manager actually *needs* to know.

Setting Up the Right Goals

You need to agree with your manager on the right goals for you. But which goals are "right"?

First, goals that you *set yourself*—or at least significantly influence—are the most motivating. So, to the extent possible, try to come up with your own goals or at least have a say on them. Don't just be passive in the process, but try to partner with your manager in setting up motivating targets for yourself, both in the short term (daily, weekly, monthly) and in the longer term (yearly). But don't automatically adopt just *any* goals your manager proposes. If some goals feel flat-out wrong or you have other clear priorities, you should try to get them adjusted.

You also want to set reasonably *challenging* goals for yourself: ambitious, but still within reach. Goals that push you and you sincerely want to reach are much better than easily reachable targets. But your goals should not be *so* hard that you have little or no chance of achieving them; then, you're just setting yourself (and your manager) up for disappointment. For example, if you're in sales, you want a sales target that is high but still within reach if you work well. An easily reachable target isn't what you want because it isn't pushing you to do your best. At the same time, an impossible target is definitely not motivating, as you wouldn't believe that you would ever be able to sell that much.

Try also to understand how *your* goals fit into the larger picture of your *team's* goals. To do that, talk with your manager about how your results contribute to your team's results. That lets you see the bigger picture behind the tasks you're working on. Besides being motivating, understanding the overall strategies helps you direct your own work in the right direction. For example, you can devise ideas or projects that support your team's goals, not just your own scope of work.

As a note, you may experience that *you* are more ambitious than your manager, especially in entry-level positions. Maybe you want to take on more challenging tasks, move faster, or try more new things than your manager allows. Instead, your manager holds you back and wants you to work on more mundane tasks than you aspire for. In that situation, the best you can do is to have patience and loyally and energetically do what you're asked to do; after all, many entry-level positions are designed that way. By doing that, you show your goodwill and good attitude—which is, anyway, more likely to move you on to more exciting work than if you sulk. Put in your best effort and do your tasks with diligence and dignity. At the same time, train your *soft skills*: remember that your hard skills are only half of what counts. The other half is your soft skills and those you can hone and polish as much as you want while you're sweating away in your entry-level position. In fact, your soft skills can be the differentiator that quickly moves you on to more inspiring and challenging work.

Agree on Your Authority

As you get increasingly more competent and confident in your job, you need to agree with your manager on which decisions you can make yourself. When you clarify in advance which categories of decisions you can make on your own, you're in a much better place to act independently and effectively. Additionally, clear agreements prevent you from overstepping your authority. So try to regularly clarify your authority (for example, in your one-on-one meetings).

Shape Your Job

Your job role usually isn't set in stone, and defining your job content isn't necessarily a top-down process that only rests with your manager. In fact, *you* can, in most jobs, *also* shape it to fit better with your natural strengths, your values, and your interests. Your power to customize your own job content is likely bigger than you think, especially as you earn goodwill for yourself with your work and your results, and as your manager understands your talents and strengths.

By customizing your job, both you and your manager benefit: you'll be more effective, more motivated, and likely stay longer in your job. That's in the interest of both of you. So don't be too modest or anxious to push for changes in your job content; instead, take responsibility for your own career. Your manager cannot do that for you because only *you* know yourself the way you do.

But *how* do you shape your job? Again, the first thing is to *do* it instead of being passive and waiting for your manager to show the way. So the first step starts in your head: by recognizing that you *can* take ownership of your job and career and actively mold it to be a better fit for you. Then, it's a process over time where you, little by little, redesign your job in two parallel ways:

1. You try to get *more* of the activities that *fit* you: you volunteer, ask for, and grab opportunities when they arise. For example, if you're an engineer and wish for more work that involves other people, you can try to *add* activities where you interact with others. Maybe you can include teaching or support in your job content. Or perhaps you can take part in customer-facing activities. Whatever it is, the idea is to actively *seek* tasks and activities that fit you.

2. You try to get *less* of the activities that *don't fit* you. Maybe you can agree to swap tasks with a colleague. Or maybe you can agree with your manager that you shouldn't do those tasks. Or that your manager can delegate them to a colleague who actually likes to do them. Alternatively, maybe the activities you don't like can be done more efficiently if you work on improving the processes.

The essential point is that shaping your job is not a one-time event but something you do gradually and progressively over time.

Performance Reviews

As a standard practice, most organizations hold formal performance evaluation conversations once per year—sometimes twice per year. These conversations also go under other names: performance appraisal, employee appraisal, performance development discussion, and other variations. The intention with performance reviews is to align expectations between you and your manager (as discussed in the previous section) and support your career development.

It's usually a formal requirement that managers hold these conversations with their direct reports (at least) once per year. And often, elaborate systems and processes are in place to facilitate and ensure the conversations actually occur. These systems and processes, managed by the HR (Human Resources) function, also store the results of the conversations and provide guidelines and templates for managers and employees to follow.

Part of the process is usually that the manager gives the employee a score (a grade, often on a 1–5 scale) on different objectives, such as "inspire trust," "deliver results," "innovation," "communication," or whatever is chosen by the organization. The employee as well gives himself or herself a score. Then, during the conversation, the manager and the employee negotiate which score is most correct (the manager has the final word), and the scores are stored in the system. These scores are important, as they may influence opportunities for training, promotions, salary, and bonuses.

How significant performance reviews are for you depends on your relationship with your manager and how good your manager is at giving feedback. If you've developed a good working relationship, these formal conversations can be mere formalities. But if you haven't developed a good working relationship and don't work much together, the performance review becomes essential. It might be the *only* occasion where you can have a deeper conversation about your goals and career development with your manager. That's not ideal and *not* the situation you want. As discussed, the best strategy is to align with your manager *often* and *informally*. You want to focus on your daily performance and on getting regular feedback. Not just once per year.

Take Performance Reviews with a Grain of Salt

Performance reviews are conducted in very different ways in different organizations. And depending on your organization and your manager, there could be some pitfalls to look out for.

First, all managers haven't necessarily been thoroughly trained in developing other people or in giving feedback. On top of that, managers' evaluations often say as much about themselves as they say about the person they evaluate: their evaluations may be *projections*. For example, if your manager is detail-oriented, he or she may be particularly observant of *your* attention to detail. Or if your manager is social and focused on building harmony in your team, he or she may look for the same traits in you and evaluate you less positively if that's not *your* strong side.

Another potential problem is that the systems and guidelines governing the performance review may limit how managers can evaluate their employees. For example, there may be a limit to how many employees can get the top score of "5"; it could be that each manager is only allowed to give a limited number of employees a score of "5" to force them to use more of the scale from 1–5. For you, that means that your score may be a *relative* performance score, not an *absolute*; your personal score may be relative to your teammates. Consequently, if you're in a strong team, getting the best scores might take relatively more than in a weak team.

Additionally, if you talk about your performance only once per year, the goals you set up for the next year often quickly lose relevancy. They risk being obsolete when you discuss them the next year. (A year is a long time when it comes to setting goals.) Thus, you may find yourself in the odd and awkward situation of trying to follow up on goals that were already obsolete shortly after your last performance review. Again, this is one of the reasons why you want to have frequent performance conversations with your manager.

So, take the performance reviews with a grain of salt: while you should—absolutely—take them seriously, you should, at the same time, be aware that this is no exact science and that it can lead to disappointments. Accept that you will not always be able to score high. When you do get a disappointing score, don't feel insulted or sad about it; instead, ask what it would take to improve your score the next time—and work toward those targets with your best efforts.

How to Manage the Performance Review

How do you get the most out of the performance review? First, you want to approach the conversation with a positive and constructive mindset. And make sure to prepare as much as possible: start your preparation some days in advance, not just the last hour before. Part of the preparation can also be to review the section on how to receive feedback in Skill 1: Building Self-Awareness. You can also freshen up on your soft skills, which can only benefit you in the meeting. As well, check up on the formal guidelines for the performance review and ask your colleagues how your manager holds these meetings.

Additionally, here are four other good practices:

1. **Influence your evaluation.** Obviously, the best way to have a good performance review is to perform well during the year! But you *can* also influence the evaluation itself: *now* is the time to talk about your good accomplishments. You don't want to undervalue yourself or be overly modest. And you *do* want to make sure your manager understands your good results (without inflating them). Especially if you don't work closely with your manager, he or she will not know the details of your work and your results. So you need to convey that information: prepare a list of the things you have done in the past year, and try to include hard facts, numbers, and nice feedback from others to support it. Use that in the meeting to convey where you've had successes. You can also send it to your manager in advance.

2. **Be future-focused.** Although you want to talk about your past accomplishments, the meeting should be predominantly about your *future*. Talk about your *future* and how it can be supported—and don't get stuck in what already *has* happened.

3. **Ask for what you want.** This is also the time to ask for what you want to make you more efficient and develop yourself—to the extent you haven't already done so during the year. You can ask for training, participation in conferences, a new position, opportunities in other parts of the organization, involvement in exciting projects, salary raises, assignments, promotions, mentoring, coaching, new tools, a new laptop, whatever you need. Don't hold back; this is the key event formally set up to discuss this. Before the meeting, prepare a prioritized list of your wishes and why you want them (to avoid forgetting anything). Obviously, you won't get everything you ask for—but what is important is that your manager knows what you want and what motivates you.

4. **Discuss the deep things.** If there's anything you're unhappy or uncomfortable with, and you don't get to talk about those issues

in your daily work, *this* is also the time to discuss it. Problems with balancing your work with your family life, career aspirations in entirely other directions, a thorny issue with a colleague, whatever. These kinds of difficult topics should also be discussed in the meeting, as they significantly influence your work life.

If Your Relationship with Your Manager Is *Not* Working

Sometimes, it seems that your relationship with your manager just won't work. If that is the case, you need to check out how others are doing with this manager: Do some of your colleagues also have these same problems? Have some people stopped working for this manager and found new jobs?

Depending on the answers to these questions, there are two ways to proceed:

1. If your colleagues generally have the same problems with this manager as you, and your team has a high employee turnover, you've likely gotten a manager who is hard to work for. In other words, a manager with low management or people skills. If your manager ignores you, distrusts you, blames you, disrespects you, is abusive, etc., despite your best intentions and efforts, it will be an uphill battle to get the relationship right. The best you can do is probably to start looking for a new position with another manager, either inside or outside of your organization.

2. Oppositely, if your colleagues are generally satisfied with your manager, you may need to think again. Are your results, in all honesty, below what they should be? Are you overreacting or misinterpreting things? Have you gotten off on the wrong foot with your manager? People's childhood experiences with authority figures—at home and at school—often greatly influence how they interact with their managers later in life. From those experiences, they have built their own strategies for dealing with authority. Some have found a good balance, whereas others have adopted dysfunctional habits of being passive and avoidant, being manipulative, or being aggressive and

rebelling. So do a little self-assessment. What is *your* experience? How do *you* deal with authority? Do *you* bring some dysfunctional habits from your past? Consequently, before you judge your relationship with your manager as dead, take a look at yourself. Because what you see in your manager could be your own projections and biases—your *past* playing games with your present. Thus, changing jobs (and manager) is not the solution: you will have to start with yourself. Talk with friends and colleagues about your situation, and maybe get help from a coach. Obviously, if you—after this introspection—still think there's no way forward, you could start looking for another job.

SKILL 9

TIME MANAGEMENT

- Clarify the expectations before you begin a new task.

- Focus on what's most important. Urgent is not necessarily the same as important.

- Take responsibility for how much you work.

Your *time* may be your most important asset at work. There's no substitute for your time; you cannot stretch it or get back the time you've already spent. You must be diligent about it. It can sometimes feel like you have *no control* over your time, that it's just consumed by your manager, colleagues, customers, administrative tasks, and frequent interruptions.

That's why it's essential to have powerful techniques to help you manage your time.

Get Organized

The most basic thing in being effective is to be—reasonably—well organized. Because if you cannot find important tools, documents, files, emails, or whatever you need, you may spend hours searching. And that's ineffective. On top of that, you may spend additional time redoing lost work or getting a replacement tool. If you're a structured person, you'll not have a problem with this. But if you're less structured, this is likely an area where you can be more effective.

For example, with emails and folders, it pays big dividends to spend a couple of hours once and for all to thoroughly think through an efficient structure and to maintain it regularly by adding new folders and archiving obsolete ones as needed. With a well-thought-out structure, you'll be able to quickly file and retrieve anything you need.

You also want to keep your email inbox under control by recurrently (at least daily) responding to and archiving emails. You can use labels and categories to group your emails to get a better overview. However, you don't want to keep emails lying in your inbox, just waiting for when you "have time" to process them. Having an inbox that grows out of control to hundreds, or thousands, of emails is inefficient and unprofessional. You simply need to have your inbox under control. Some people even advocate completely emptying the inbox at least once per day.

Similarly, use your organization's calendar system to organize your workday and avoid double-bookings. And use reminders so you won't forget meetings or appointments.

Finally, keep your tools, instruments, office supplies, or whatever material things you need organized: systematically arrange and find a place for everything. And, at the end of the day, before you go home, clean up and put things back in place so that when you come to work the next day, you get a fresh start with all your stuff in the right places.

Eliminate Distractions

If you're frequently interrupted by unnecessary distractions, it affects your productivity and wastes your time. And it's all too easy to get distracted. The best way to eliminate distractions is to close, turn off, silence, unsubscribe, or uninstall as many things as possible that compete for your attention and interrupt your work. Here are some practical ideas:

- On your computer, turn off email alerts and desktop notifications. Don't let email or social media interrupt and distract you every time you get a new message or update—limit yourself to checking them only a few times per day, as necessary for your work (more about this later).

- Don't subscribe to emails or newsletters unless you actually *use them*—and unsubscribe if you find that you don't look at or use the information.

- Turn off as many notifications and alerts on your phone as possible; keep only those you absolutely need for your work. And, if feasible in your job, put your phone on silent.

- Use noise-canceling headphones.

You can also reduce the temptation to distract yourself by physically removing distracting objects. For example, you can move your phone physically out of reach when you don't need it; that little trick alone can save you many distractions. This is also called the "two-meter rule": remove the distraction two meters away.

Taking in New Tasks or Projects: Saying Yes

You need to be clear about what exactly you're asked to do when you get a new assignment or say yes to do something, as assignments and requests may be incomplete or not carefully prepared. That often leads to wasted time and work that has to be redone. Therefore, a good handing over of tasks and assignments is absolutely crucial. When you're the receiver of the request, *you* have a big part of the responsibility to make sure that you actually work on the right things.

So, when you take in a new task or project, you should clarify the expectations before you begin. It doesn't matter who the request comes from; you want to ask for clarification if there's anything vague or confusing, or something you don't understand. Even if it feels uncomfortable to admit that you don't understand, it's better to swallow your pride and ask for clarification until you fully understand what you're being asked. Because the alternative is worse: you could risk working in a wrong direction. Thus, if the request is unclear, you need to work with the requester to improve it. That's also in the requester's interest, who may not have given the request due consideration before asking you. Actually, when you ask for clarification and more information before you say yes, you're helping *both* of you.

So, what does a good yes look like? Basically, it consists of four pieces of necessary information:

1. **Who is requesting it?** This isn't always obvious; for example, if the requester is more than one person, like in "We would like you to . . ." or "The architecture team wants . . ." In such cases, which person should you then ask for clarifications? Who will decide when it's done? You need to know who is ultimately responsible for the request.

2. **What is being asked?** You need to know what kind of action or deliverable is being requested, and you need to have it sufficiently detailed to estimate the amount of work. Ask for samples, templates, examples, and previous versions to help you better understand what's being asked.

3. **When does it have to be finalized?** You need to understand the time frame of the request. Note that ASAP (As Soon As Possible) is not useful because that can mean different things to different people. Always ask when exactly the work has to be done.

4. **What are the *acceptance criteria*?** How will you know when you are "done"? This is called "Definition of Done" in the software world because it can be ambiguous what "done" really means! Is it when the programming is done? When the testing is done? And what kind of testing? The deliverable (the software) will look the same in these cases, but what is an acceptable standard could be a matter of interpretation. Thus, if there is any doubt, try to get to a clear agreement about what the acceptance criteria are.

For most tasks and assignments, except the smallest, consider writing down *your* understanding of what's being requested, using this structure of the four pieces of necessary information. Be as clear and concise as you can and then share it with the requester. End with *asking for confirmation*, for example: "Is this correctly understood?" That way, you significantly reduce the risk of costly and time-consuming misunderstandings.

Estimating

When you get a request, you usually also want to estimate how much time you'll spend on it. The *requester* needs to know it (if you're part of a project or your time is being invoiced), and *you* need to know so you can plan your time.

Estimating isn't always easy, but that isn't an argument for not doing it. Having some form of an estimate is much better than none. Of course, an estimate *is* merely an educated guess, so accept that you won't always get it right. Don't be overly optimistic and assume that things go smoothly, but add a buffer to account for unforeseen events, mistakes, and all the little things that always add up in the end. Because what you need is a realistic estimate.

To improve your estimation skills, you can note down both your *estimate* and the *actual* time used. When comparing the actuals with the estimates, you'll get a feeling for whether you typically under- or overestimate. If you make that a habit, you will, over time, improve your estimation skills.

Prioritizing Your Tasks

Knowing which tasks and activities you need to do—your "yeses"—how do you prioritize them?

First, use a to-do list. A continually updated to-do list is a powerful tool to manage your tasks and align with your manager, teammates, project manager, or whoever you work closely with. With a to-do list, you can immediately note things down you have to do, which frees your mind from remembering them. It doesn't matter how you make your to-do list—on a piece of paper, in a file on your computer, or in a dedicated app—what's important is that you're systematic about it.

But don't put *everything* on your to-do list; if a task is tiny, it's more efficient to just do it immediately. An excellent way to remember this is the "two-minute rule": If something takes less than two minutes, do it immediately! This practical rule lets you instantly clear small actions off your table—for instance, giving someone a quick reply.

Oppositely, you don't want too *big* tasks on your to-do list. If a task is too big, it's unmanageable. Consequently, big tasks have to be broken down into smaller ones that each can be a separate item on your to-do list. For example, if you have a project to complete or a report to write that you estimate to take one month, you have to break it down into much more manageable chunks. Just dividing a report into its individual sections can be a great help.

Do the Most Important Task *First*

Next, you need to prioritize your to-do list; don't skip prioritizing just because you think you're "too busy"! Doing your tasks in the order they come in—or in the order you feel best about—isn't professional. You have to focus on what's most important. Because you can easily be *busy* without *achieving* much—if you're working hard on the *wrong* things.

A simple and valuable prioritization technique is the *80/20 rule*. It says that—broadly speaking—80 percent of the value typically comes from 20 percent of the activities. Consequently, you need to focus on the few high-value activities (the 20 percent) that create the most value (the 80 percent). Or, said in another way, there is much more value in your most important activities, making it essential to identify and commit to doing *them* first.

It's also useful to distinguish between the *important* versus the *urgent*. Sometimes requests that seem urgent aren't really important—for example, if an impatient customer or colleague keeps asking you for something. Then it can be tempting to just give in and do what the impatient person is asking for. But that's the wrong choice if more important tasks are pushed aside as a consequence. Likewise, the really important activities aren't always urgent, at least not initially. For example, the most uncertain and difficult tasks may not be the most urgent, but they may be the ones making all the difference. So you need to be careful not to let the urgent trump the important. The way to do that is to actively seek out the most *important* items on your to-do list and make them your top priorities so they don't get pushed aside by the seemingly unending *urgent* tasks. If you're in doubt about what really is the most important, you can always consult with your manager or senior colleagues.

As an example, let's assume that you have your to-do list in front of you, each item with a time estimate. Let's say that you have ten small tasks of one to two hours, four medium tasks of four to eight hours, and one big task that you estimate to be twenty hours but haven't been able to further break down. The smaller tasks are routine, and you're pretty sure you can do them without experiencing any problems. And you believe the medium tasks are also manageable. But you're uncertain about the big task, as you haven't tried it before and think it may be difficult. Take a moment to consider: In which order would you make these tasks?

Many people would start with the easiest tasks—because it feels good to *produce* something, and they can quickly report progress: "I've already completed seven tasks." But unfortunately, that's the wrong order. The right order is to start with the most uncertain and challenging task. Because the uncertainty can make it a significant problem: What if a closer examination shows that it's not twenty hours but fifty? Or one hundred? Then a project, your team, or someone depending on this task could be in serious trouble. And *that* makes it the most important task and your first priority. So, start with the big task to better understand what it encompasses; by doing that, you bring down the uncertainty. You could start with three hours of concentrated work as soon as possible to get a grip on it. Then you may find that it isn't as difficult as you thought—or just the opposite, that it's a significant challenge. In both cases, you have much better information now, and you can proceed all the wiser.

Of course, this example is simplified because some of the smaller tasks may be urgent (someone may be waiting for them) and therefore need to be done first. Still, the critical point is to avoid the trap of procrastinating the most challenging tasks and (instead) doing the easy ones first.

Saying No

Your to-do list is usually under constant attack from new requests and new and seemingly urgent matters. And you need to accommodate *some* of them into your to-do list and reshuffle your priorities. But you also have to say no to some things, or you may be swamped with more work than you have time for.

Obviously, saying no isn't the first thing you want to do when you're new in a job, but it's a vital skill when you've built some competence and gained some credibility. Because then, inevitably, more work will come to you—and then you *will* have to say no to some things. That may be both big and small requests, but often the many smaller asks are the most problematic. It's easy to say yes to spend five, fifteen, or thirty minutes on small requests, but at the end of the day, they may have added up to a significant amount of time spent on things that, in reality, weren't important or urgent. Or things that weren't even your responsibility. Maybe those things were *nice* or *interesting*, or something that you felt *obliged* to do but didn't really want to do. That way, as a result of what's called the "tyranny of small decisions," your workday can gradually drift away into waste.

In any case, it's often difficult to say no; saying no can feel uncomfortable. It's much easier to say yes. When you say yes, you make other people happy, and it *feels* good. But you may be saying yes for the *wrong reasons*—for example, if you say yes to be seen as competent or in control, or because you want to avoid an interpersonal conflict. These are not professional reasons to say yes. What to say yes (and no) to shouldn't be determined by psychological reasons but should, instead, be based on sound business reasoning and the common purpose. Saying no doesn't mean that you reject the *person* who's asking you—only that you reject the *request*. It's a *professional* decision, not a personal one. Saying yes to too many things will lead to delays, disappointments, people being let down, and the risk of getting stressed. Saying yes when you should have said no has consequences—usually *worse* than the consequences of saying no in the first place.

How to Say No

First, saying no becomes easier if you think about what it really is you want to accomplish: Which things do you *most* want to do? What are the *big-impact* things on your to-do list, the things that *really* matter? When you keep your big-impact things in mind, they—mentally—help you push the less important into "nos." It is, pure and simple, a matter of focus: the less time you spend on less important activities, the more time you'll be able to spend on the most important. Focusing, invariably, means saying no to some things. Here are some ways to say no, depending on *you* and on *the request*:

- **You are not *permitted* to do it.** First, consider if the person asking you is even permitted to ask you to do things or if the request goes against your organization's policies or procedures or against your manager's instructions. In these cases, you have to either say no or ask your manager for permission.

- **You *cannot* do it.** You can say no when you don't have the time, knowledge, or skills to do what is asked. If you don't have the time, that's it. And if you're not qualified, you shouldn't accept (although you might if preparation or education can be included so you actually *will* be sufficiently qualified).

- **You *should not* do it.** Sometimes people ask you to do things because they're busy with their own high priorities, or because it's simply convenient for them to have you do it. But that may conflict with *your* own high priorities. In that case, you have to make a decision: "Should I really do this? Or is this one of the many but small decisions that may slowly eat away my day?" Of course, you want to give a helping hand—in line with good team behavior—but you also have to keep a watchful eye on your top priorities, your truly important work. So, while this isn't as clear-cut as saying no because you cannot do it or are not permitted to do it, you have to weigh the request and say no if you have more important work and shouldn't be doing this.

- **You will *answer later*.** Sometimes you cannot decide here and now if you can fulfill a request or not. Maybe you need time to assess the situation and look at your other priorities on your to-do list before deciding. Or perhaps you want to ask your manager or seek advice from a senior colleague. Then you can respond, "Let me think about it and get back to you on Monday." Note that you should commit to giving the requester an answer by a *specified time*; then, he or she can plan accordingly.

- **You believe that doing it is *not right*.** Sometimes you're asked to do something you disagree with. Maybe you're asked to implement a design you believe is flawed or treat a patient in a way you have an issue with. In that case, it's okay to say no and have a dialogue about what would be a better way (maybe including your manager).

- **You *compromise*.** Sometimes a compromise can be the best way to deal with a request you don't have time for. Maybe it makes sense that you do *some part* of what's requested, but not *all*. For example, if you're invited to a long meeting, you may agree to only attend the part of the meeting where you are a necessary participant. Or you can make a counteroffer: "I cannot do A, but I can do B." For example, "I cannot make the report, but I can offer to pull the data out for you." With this approach, you basically negotiate a different kind of no that is still of value to the requester but less time-consuming for you.

- **You suggest *someone else* who can do it.** If one or more of your colleagues are better qualified or have more time, you may propose that the requester asks them instead. For example, you could answer, "Try asking Sara or Thomas. They're both qualified, and I believe they may have time now."

Now, with a clear understanding of your reason for saying no, you need to say so *clearly* and *straightforwardly*. You also want to explain your reason for saying no, as this gives the requester a better understanding of your situation and, thus, hopefully, avoids conflict or resentment between you. You should not make excuses; just explain the reasoning behind your "no." It doesn't have to be a long story, just a genuinely valid reason. You can say, "Sorry, I can't help you with that. I don't have the time, as I'm working on X." Say it clearly and firmly to avoid misunderstandings while also being calm and polite.

Working Effectively

With distractions under control, having said yes and no the right way, and your work prioritized, how do you then *work* effectively? The following best practices can help you out.

Do One Thing at a Time

Working on several things at the same time wastes your concentration by forcing you to spend energy on starting and restarting tasks and keeping track of everything. So juggling many things simultaneously isn't anything to be proud of. Instead, to the extent possible, aim for uninterrupted blocks of time where you can concentrate on only one thing and get momentum on that.

The best way to obtain this is to *plan* your workdays instead of just letting them *happen*. As much as you can, you want to be in control of your days. For example, when you need uninterrupted time blocks to focus on something challenging, schedule time for that and block it off from other activities. You can also tell your nearest colleagues that you'll be busy for that period and would prefer not to be interrupted. Most people will understand and respect that. Again, eliminate distractions and don't answer phone calls or text messages during your uninterrupted time blocks.

A useful variation is to *timebox* your work, which simply means that you decide in advance how much time you'll spend on a task (for instance, three hours).

This technique is especially helpful if you're a bit perfectionistic and tend to overdo things, because you set a limit for yourself. You say to yourself, "I'll set aside three hours for this, and then it must be finished."

Finish What You Start

Try to *finish* each task before you move on to the next thing. Concentrate on one thing and one thing only, dig in, and push through until the finish line. You really don't want to set work aside to "finish it later" if you're close to being finished. Because then you lose momentum by unnecessarily switching back and forth between tasks. If a task is too big to finish in one session, break it down into subtasks that can be completed in one uninterrupted time block.

There is one exception to this advice: If you get stuck, you may be better off doing something else for a while and then return to your first task later with a fresh perspective.

Work on Your Most Difficult Tasks When You're Most Effective

All your hours aren't equally productive. Even though one hour (obviously) is one hour in *duration*, you may be twice, or thrice, as *productive* or *creative* in your best hours of the day. Everybody knows this phenomenon: sometimes we're energetic and bright, and other times less so (or much less so).

For many people, the most productive time of day is in the morning. Whatever it is for you, your most productive hours are when you should work on your *most challenging* tasks. So, to the extent possible, try to schedule and work with your most difficult tasks during your best hours of the day. Don't work with routine or easy tasks; reserve those superpower hours for your most complex and demanding work.

And, to *stay* effective, remember to take a break now and then to renew your energy. The breaks don't have to be lengthy to be effective; even just a few minutes—regularly—can be enough to maintain your focus and performance.

Produce the Right Quality

Another key to personal effectiveness is to aim for the right quality. But what does that actually mean? What is the *right* quality? On the one hand, you obviously don't want to produce too *low* quality; that's not effective, as your work will then need to be redone or have severe consequences for other people (for example, if you're in the medical field).

On the other hand, you don't want to produce too *high* quality if it isn't needed. At a certain point, each extra minute or hour spent on something will start to yield less value than if you considered the task "done" and started on the next one instead. Especially people with a perfectionistic tendency should take care not to waste time producing unneeded quality. Here are some examples:

- Perfecting a presentation, a report, or a piece of code to the point where no one cares about the difference (e.g., spending ten hours perfecting something when five hours would be sufficient).

- Answering questions with more detail than what is asked for. For instance, answering a simple yes/no question with a long explanation.

- Producing parts to a higher tolerance than needed.

If you're in doubt about what quality is needed, *ask* the person who has requested the work from you. Let's say you've made a report and now wonder how much time you should spend formatting it. Then you can ask, "How do you want it formatted?" You may get very different answers like, "It's going to our new customer, so it needs to be nicely formatted" or "Just the raw numbers, please, as it's only for me and I don't care about the formatting."

Check Early and Often That You're on the Right Track

When you're working on a task or project, you want to avoid going in a wrong direction. And the best way to make sure you're on the right track is to *check* early and often with the person who has requested the work, such as your manager, a project manager, a colleague, a customer.

So don't wait until you have almost completed your work before checking with the requester. Even if you have taken in the task with due diligence (using the four pieces of necessary information: who, what, when, and acceptance criteria), the task may be hard to explain, or there could be misunderstandings or missing information. So you want to make sure that you're working in the right direction as early as possible. For example, you can share your early thoughts and ideas or show a draft or sample. Don't be embarrassed that it isn't perfect—that's the whole idea. Things don't have to be complete before you can start sharing them with others to get input and direction. Think about it this way: by checking, you'll reach your results *quicker*, and they'll probably be *better*.

Handle Small Tasks in Batches

The last practice is to deal with small tasks in batches. That may be processing emails, returning phone calls, replying to messages, filing, networking, or updating administrative systems. You shouldn't process tasks like these continually as they come in. You'd be interrupted all the time! Instead, the most efficient way to handle these many but small tasks is to "batch" them together in blocks. For example, you might set aside three sessions per day to check and answer emails, messages, and phone calls (or whatever fits with your job).

How Much Should You Work?

Working long hours often pays in creating good results and advancing one's career, but there's a limit. And beyond that limit, *more* work is *not* leading to better results but, instead, to adverse effects for oneself and one's family. Creativity goes down, exhaustion sets in, and tempers get shorter. And only *you* can draw the line where the limit is; it's a personal thing.

So you have to ask yourself a simple (but profound) question: "What is *my* definition of success?" Is it pursuing a particular professional path that you've been dreaming about? Having a prestigious career with a good salary? Caring for other people and making them happy? Having enough time outside of work to pursue a hobby or sport? Raising a family and seeing work as a second priority? Making a difference in the world or in your community? (You may want to check the work values in Skill 2: Setting Goals again.)

These are deeply personal choices, so this book cannot tell you how much to work. But it can suggest some techniques to help you *set* the limits. And setting limits *is* accepted—or even expected—in most organizations as long as you're doing it appropriately and are otherwise doing a good job.

If you have a tendency to work too much—compared to your personal definition of success—here are some techniques to help you set limits.

Decide When to Leave Work

Unless something extraordinary happens, *decide* when to leave work (or stop working if you work from home); for example, 5:00 P.M. When you've already decided in advance when to stop, it's easier to do it because you've got your mind set on it. It's also easier to focus on the most important things during your workday because you know your time runs out at 5:00 P.M. With that decision clearly made, you won't fall into the trap of "just one more" short-term task. One more email. One more meeting. One more client. One more phone call. The "one more" will have to wait until the next day. And if you have a difficult manager who wants you to stay much longer than what is reasonable, you can (calmly and politely) stand your ground.

When You're Not Working, Don't Work

In the evenings, on the weekend, during holidays, decide when you work and where your limit is when you *don't* work. For example, you could choose not to check email (or do any other job-related activity) from Friday after work to Sunday evening (where you could check email to get ready for Monday morning). During those forty-eight hours, you give yourself a complete rest. The same for vacations and holidays. Then, stick to it. Of course, no set rule can or should be made for this, as it depends entirely on your job and circumstances. The point is to make sure you create *some* work-free zones where you can completely wind down.

To align expectations with your manager and colleagues, make it clear and transparent to them when exactly your work-free zones are. Then there should be no misunderstandings. Agree with them on how they *can* contact you in case of an emergency or a crisis—for example, that they can contact you by phone or text message.

If you decide to do some work anyway—for example, responding to some emails during your weekend—remember that you don't have to *send* them immediately. You can save your emails as drafts and then wait to send them until Monday morning. That way, you avoid giving other people the expectation that you work and accept being disturbed in your work-free zones.

Plan Buffer Time

Don't schedule your days too tightly. If you book every hour of your workday with activities and meetings, you won't have buffer time for interruptions and unforeseen events. And that's pretty unrealistic in most jobs.

So how do you handle working in an environment with plenty of unplanned events, disruptions, and crises? You *plan* for it—by scheduling *buffers* into your workday. For example, if you have an eight-hour workday, you could choose to plan only six of those hours and keep the last two hours open for unexpected things, including socializing with colleagues. If nothing pops up, those two hours are just available for your important work.

Allow Yourself to Regenerate after a Busy Period

Every job will have its busy periods. For example, accounting usually has busy periods every quarter when the financial statements have to be ready. It's okay, and often expected, that you work harder than usual during these periods.

But after such a period, you need to slow down and unwind because you *cannot* continually work in your highest gear. Think about athletes: they all need to rest after a peak performance to let their bodies regenerate. If they don't do that, their performance will drop or they'll get injured. It's the same for work, so allow yourself a quieter time after a stressful period to recharge your batteries. Don't fall for the temptation to jump directly to the next peak performance without having had any rest in-between. Because there will always be a new peak performance nearing: a new project is started, a crisis appears, a colleague resigns, and you have to take over. Consequently, jumping from peak to peak—with no rest in-between—is a recipe for stress and burnout. And then you're definitely *not* effective anymore.

Challenge Unnecessarily Demanding Self-Talk

Sometimes, it's not your manager, customer, patient, or colleague who demands too much work from you. Sometimes it's *you* who is too hard on *you*. It's your own self-talk that's unnecessarily rigid or demanding. Such self-talk often includes words like "must," "can't," "have to," "should," etc. For example, "I *can't* leave it to others; I *have to* do it myself." The problem with this kind of self-talk is that it usually isn't true: you *can* take responsibility and decide *differently*. That is within your circle of control. You don't "have to" do anything. You just may not like the consequences or may fear that they're worse than they really are.

One great way to challenge demanding self-talk is to substitute the demanding words with the word "*choose*." That changes the example to "I *choose* to do it myself." When formulated that way, the situation is now a *choice*, making it clear that there are other options.

Another way is to imagine that the person you're doing work for is speaking to you like you're speaking to yourself. For example, suppose he or she said to you, "You cannot go home before you finish! Your children may be missing you, but I *demand* that you finish this first!" When you do this thought experiment, it's probably clear the requestor of your work would never speak to you like that and it is *you* who is the most demanding part. In reality, it may be perfectionism, a desire to be accepted, or some other psychological reason that's driving you. And not the requester of your work.

SKILL 10

DECISION-MAKING

- Know your decision-making authority.

- Decisions don't have to be perfect.

- Make use of people's differences to make better decisions.

You cannot *not* make decisions; making decisions is an integral part of your job. In a typical workday, you'll likely make many decisions, both small and big. Some of them can be difficult and involve weighing a lot of information and deciding between several options of which none may stand out as ideal. So it isn't always easy to make decisions. That's why good decision-making skills are crucial in many jobs and highly valued by professional organizations. This chapter goes through some best practices, as well as some traps to avoid.

First, Follow Your Organization's Guidelines

In most organizations, the same types of problems and decisions have been seen time and time again. And the accumulated knowledge and experience have been standardized into rules, policies, guidelines, and templates that align and professionalize how employees make decisions. For example:

- People in the front line have guidelines for how to respond to complaints.

- Bank employees have policies they must follow when processing loan applications.

- Doctors have guidelines for diagnosis and treatment at their disposal.

The point is that in most jobs, many decisions are governed by guidelines that you can (or must) follow when making decisions. In reality, the room for anyone to make individual and creative decisions may be limited. Many decisions may already have been taken in creating the *frame conditions* for your job.

So, when it comes to making decisions, the first thing you need to know is what your decision-making authority is. What policies and guidelines exist? What are your constraints and boundaries? Which decisions can you make yourself, and which must be handled by others?

For example, if you work as a junior officer on a ship, the decision to deviate from the route to avoid bad weather may not be yours but should be made by the captain. If you work as a programmer, some decisions are for the architecture or security teams, not for you. Or, if your work involves money, you can only approve transactions up to a certain amount; above that amount, they must be approved by a higher management level.

Decision-Making Best Practices

Within the frame conditions set out by your organization's policies and guidelines, you have the discretion to make your own decisions. Consider the following best practices to help you.

Get Another Opinion

The first practice is—simply—to get another opinion. Before you decide, consider asking for someone else's view to get a different perspective. That's a good practice, both when you're in doubt and, as well, when you feel certain (because you may have made an error of judgment). To get qualified and unbiased advice, think about *who* you ask and *how* you ask:

- **Who:** Try to get the opinion of the *most experienced* people, including people who are senior to you. Their deep experience is often invaluable, so they can give you quick and qualified input. And don't avoid asking those you suspect hold different viewpoints than yourself (even though it may feel uncomfortable). Because you're not looking for confirmation but for qualified opinions and a broad set of views.

- **How:** Accurately describe the situation and the decision you're facing. Then ask for advice in a way that *avoids biasing* the other person with your own preconceived opinions. Don't first tell the other person about your own ideas or tentative conclusions. Avoid leading questions; ask open-ended questions. Ask, for example, "How would you approach this?" Note that if you're asking your manager for advice, *you* should still assume responsibility for the decision. Asking for advice or an opinion is not something you do to avoid accountability.

Sometimes, Slow Down

If you're in too much haste or under time pressure, you may overlook important information or disregard or suppress conflicting information just because you're in a hurry. But haste is frequently the enemy of good decisions. You often don't *have to* make decisions as quickly as you feel; in fact, you may be experiencing a false sense of urgency. To test that, ask yourself, "Do I really have to make this decision *right now*?" Maybe it isn't really *so* urgent, and you can slow down and give yourself more time to go through a more solid decision-making process.

Slowing down is also vital if you're emotional, maybe angry or anxious, or panicking. Then the old advice to "sleep on it" is the right thing to do, and you can resume your decision-making the next day when you've calmed down.

Decisions Don't Have to Be Perfect

The 80/20 rule also applies to decisions: some require your full attention and a thorough process, while others can be made faster and more pragmatically. Which decisions to spend the most attention on depend on how significant the consequences of the decision are and whether or not it can be reversed.

For example, if you work in digital marketing, many of your decisions are reversible and not highly consequential. You can change pictures, prices, texts, headlines, and channels almost instantly, or at least in a matter of hours or days. In reality, you can experiment quite a lot with your marketing mix without any severe or long-term consequences.

In all jobs, many decisions are like this; if they turn out to be wrong, it isn't the end of the world. So if you find it difficult or frightening to make a decision, you may have to lower your expectations, especially if you have a tendency to be perfectionistic. Don't be intimidated by making decisions, because they don't have to be *perfect*. Indeed, spending too much time on a decision (and maybe, ending up making no decision at all) is often worse than making a suboptimal decision. *Doing something* usually trumps indecision.

Consider the following tips to counter unnecessarily overthinking a decision that really doesn't need it.

First, allow yourself to settle for "good enough." If you don't have to make an *optimal* decision, but only a *good enough* decision to meet your criteria, you can save a lot of time and effort. When you generate alternatives for your decision, just search until you have a few that satisfy your criteria (maybe two or three) and evaluate only them. Let's say you're deciding on a company that can provide a transport service for your organization. Then you probably don't want to check *all* transportation providers in your city to find the very best. That makes no sense. Instead, you want to stop your search when you have found a few companies that satisfy your criteria. Then you evaluate only those and make a decision. That's "good enough" for the purpose.

Second, allow yourself to make a decision even when you're not 100 percent sure. Because if you go for *certainty*, you may never finish your decision-making process. Risk and uncertainty are (almost) always part of making decisions, and you'll rarely be able to completely eliminate them. You have to accept that there's a risk your decision will be wrong. And if you make *many* decisions, you'll have to accept that *some* of them *will* be wrong! Consequently, you have to acknowledge that you'll sometimes make choices that turn out bad. That's a natural part of making decisions, not a reflection of your competence.

But then, *how* certain should you be before you decide? That, of course, depends on the decision, but going for too high a certainty is not effective, as, at some point, you'll just be wasting your time perfecting a decision that's already as good as it needs to be. Then it's better to make the decision and accept that there's a risk it might turn out wrong.

Third, you can apply a bit of pressure on yourself if you find it difficult to decide. A good way to do so is to give yourself a time limit for the decision. Ask yourself, "How long will I allow myself to make this decision?" and then stick to that.

Use Data and Hard Facts

Some decisions are made on too loose a basis, made impulsively, or overly affected by emotions. One of the best ways to counter that is to deliberately use data and hard facts.

That starts at the beginning of the decision-making process by taking a step back and *not trusting your first impulse*. Instead, seek out more options and back them up with hard facts before deciding. And when you search for information, use *objective* data. Don't just use the information that comes quickly to mind; it may be biased by, for instance, what you heard most recently or what is easiest to recall.

For example, if you're a category manager in charge of a range of products, you want to let the *numbers* speak (sales, margin, inventory turns, cross-sales, etc.). You don't want to be too affected by which products you personally like, which salespeople you get along with the best, or which demos you most recently had. Instead, let the statistics guide your decision-making. Most organizations also have decision-support systems that are well developed and capable. Use them to assist your decisions, or ask for training if you don't know how to use them.

For the more consequential decisions, consider making a *pros-and-cons* list (advantages and disadvantages). List *all* the pros and cons you can think of—not just the big and obvious ones—to give you a good overview of the forces influencing the decision. By *systematically* listing them, you counter any tendencies you may have to be biased for—or against—certain alternatives over others. In many cases, you should also assign a weight to each of the pros and cons because they will not be equally important (for instance, on a scale of 1–5). Now, with your alternatives listed and the pros and cons weighed and backed by good data, you're ready to make your decisions. This kind of documentation is also often what you need when presenting your decision to others—for example, your manager. It shows your reasoning and that you've been deliberate and systematic in your decision-making process.

Consider Opportunity Costs

When evaluating your different decision alternatives against each other, it's good practice to also consider the potential benefits you *miss out on*. Because choosing something invariably implies *giving up* something else at the same time: resources, time, or money that could have been spent on something else of potentially higher value. In that sense, opportunity costs are the hidden costs associated with *not* making *another* decision. Forgetting opportunity costs can skew your decisions and make you overestimate how attractive the best option is.

You can factor in opportunity costs by asking yourself, "Is there a *better* way to use these resources, this time, or this money?" When thinking this way, it's easier to remember to include opportunity costs in your considerations. For example, if you decide to spend your day on A, you're *not* spending it on B or C. Therefore, B and C are opportunity costs.

Opportunity costs also influence most of the decisions that managers make, as they always have to weigh what *else* they could have done with the resources they have. They seldom have the luxury of seeing decisions as stand-alone only; they usually have to see their choices compared to other alternatives. They have to see their decisions from a larger perspective. For example, if you have an idea for an investment, there's no guarantee that your manager will approve it just because it's a *good* investment. Because if there's a *better* way to invest your organization's resources, that should be prioritized higher.

Challenge Your Assumptions

Decisions often turn out wrong because people don't think through what assumptions they're making. Sometimes, that leads them to make overly *optimistic* decisions that can only work if several unrealistic assumptions all hold. Oppositely, it can lead them to make too *pessimistic* assumptions, making them dismiss otherwise sound decisions.

A typical situation is when people are overly optimistic when estimating how long a project will take to complete. For example, they may assume that the resources and people the project needs will be available—exactly when needed. And that people produce good quality without any errors. And that outside providers will deliver without delays. And so on. But anyone who has been involved in projects of just moderate complexity knows that such assumptions rarely hold.

Therefore, in any consequential decisions, you have to know which assumptions you're making and whether they're realistic.

The first step is to *identify* which assumptions you're making. That isn't necessarily easy, as your assumptions may be things you take for granted without even realizing it. So try to be imaginative. Write down all the assumptions you can think of. Be specific. Also, get help from experienced colleagues to come up with even more assumptions (that you could have overlooked). People who are, by nature, a bit skeptical are good at this. Don't fear their judgment; instead, appreciate their experience because the earlier you can identify any wrong assumptions, the better.

When you've identified your assumptions, you need to *test* them. Start with the ones that will have the most severe consequences if they don't hold true. Here are some ideas on how you can test your assumptions:

- Get assurances. For example, if your decision's success depends on other people's or other companies' deliverables, you cannot always assume they will deliver what they said, when they said. So double-check it.

- Challenge the information your assumptions are based on. Is it hard facts, or merely anecdotal "evidence"? Is the source or person credible? Does some kind of proof exist? As a simple example, if you're booking a meeting room that you've never been in before, go and see it for yourself. *Is* it actually large enough for the number of participants you have planned, and *does* it have the equipment it's supposed to have?

- Make a real-world test. For instance, if you work in marketing, a market survey. Or if you work in medicine, a blood test.

- If you've made estimates, challenge them (for example, estimates of sales, cost, volume, time, resources, consumption, etc.). Ask yourself if the high and low ends of your estimates really *are* the highest/lowest. Or could they possibly be *even* higher or *even* lower? Again, seek help from experienced colleagues to challenge your estimates.

Don't Let Decisions Be Influenced by Sunk Costs

Finally, be aware that you don't fall for the "sunk costs" trap. Once a decision has been made, people often hold on to it simply because they've invested time, money, or effort in it and abandoning it would imply that they've made a mistake and wasted their time and resources. But, in reality, that cost is *already* sunk: the time, effort, and money cannot be retrieved. In a way, sunk costs are like when you've bought a pair of ill-fitting shoes and only found out after you started using them. Your investment in the shoes is a sunk cost, and you can just as well sell them or get rid of them. It makes no sense to keep them if they don't fit.

A problem with this is that the longer it goes on, the worse it becomes. Imagine that you've made a wrong decision. But when you found out, you didn't abandon it and cut your losses; instead, you held on to it and defended your decision and spent even more time trying to prove it right and save face. However, things didn't change for the better, and now you have (again) invested more time and resources—and maybe personal prestige. That's the sunk-cost trap in a nutshell: it can easily escalate into wasting more and more time, money, and energy.

From a decision-making point of view, *future choices shouldn't be influenced by sunk costs.* Consequently, don't be too proud or vain to change your mind when you realize that your first decision was wrong. Admit the erroneous decision, cut your losses, and move on.

Making Decisions with Others

Some other dynamics kick in when you make decisions with others—a teammate, your whole team, a project team, or a group of colleagues. Now people can *elevate* each other: more minds on the same decision bring together different competencies and provide more brainpower and perspectives. With a cliché, 2 plus 2 can become 5. However, negative group dynamics may instead *hinder* effective decision-making, and then 2 plus 2 may end up being 3 (or less).

Therefore, when making decisions with others, it's necessary to constructively employ people's differences. As mentioned, we all have different natural strengths, personalities, and values. In short, we are quite different! And not least when we make decisions together, those differences can show up and make the joint decision-making process challenging—if we don't know how to appreciate and manage them. The differences appear as different *preferences*:

- Some people prefer analysis, logic, and technical aspects—whereas others prefer concern for people, relationships, and emotional impacts.

- Some people prefer creative, new, and innovative solutions—whereas others prefer practical, tried-and-tested ones.

- Some people prefer openly sharing their unfiltered thoughts and ideas—whereas others prefer thinking things through first before sharing with others.

- Some people prefer making quick decisions—whereas others prefer keeping decisions open, getting more information, and staying flexible.

- Some people happily accept risk—whereas others are naturally risk-averse.

Everyone is a mix of these different preferences. Note that, as they are *preferences*, it doesn't mean that people cannot see the other perspectives—just that their initial, spontaneous reaction will be in the direction of their preferred way of thinking. You've probably been in situations where these different preferences have caused tensions and misunderstandings. However, instead of letting them be a source of conflict, the best way to deal with them is to leverage them to make better decisions. The different preferences *complement* each other by offering different perspectives, all of which are valid. They shouldn't compete against each other.

So try to appreciate the differences as constructive. When taking part in group decision-making, the best way to do that is to start with yourself. If you think that other people in the group are too emotional/rational, fast/slow, outspoken/quiet, and so on, take a step back and remind yourself that these differences aren't necessarily bad or are a sign that there's anything wrong with them. Remind yourself that *your* way to approach decisions isn't the only way, and look for the contribution and value of the other approaches.

Practical Techniques When Making Decisions with Others

Sometimes, different kinds of negative group dynamics can make it challenging to make decisions together. People not only have different decision-making preferences but also different competencies, backgrounds, ages, and positions in the hierarchy. They may not act professionally—for example, they may exhibit the *bad* behaviors mentioned in Skill 5: Professional Behaviors, especially if they're under pressure. There may be power plays or hidden agendas. Or people who try to dominate the agenda. Or people who just want to survive and don't want to speak their genuine opinion.

Such dynamics aren't easily managed. Likewise, your capacity to influence things may be limited. And it's not your responsibility to fix the problems on your own. However, a number of techniques can be helpful, and you don't have to be in a leading role to use them. These techniques aim at ensuring that all ideas and alternatives are objectively and critically evaluated and that everybody is heard to the extent possible. Note that all the good team behaviors also apply when making decisions together. The below six techniques are simply a supplement to that:

1. **Recruit differing opinions:** If people in a group are too like-minded, they can easily overlook or dismiss valid alternatives or make biased decisions. So if you're involved in forming a decision-making group, try to include people with differing backgrounds, skills, and opinions. Let's say you have a decision to make, and you want to bring together some colleagues to discuss it. Then you should avoid inviting only people you expect will agree with you and support your preconceived ideas; you want to *also* include people who represent different viewpoints and have differing goals. You don't want to create a group that's merely an echo chamber of your own opinions.

2. **Gather opinions independently and before people share their thoughts with each other:** If you gather people's views independently instead of in a shared session where they can influence each other, everyone has an equal opportunity to participate, regardless of

position, background, and decision-making style. For example, agree that someone first collects all input and ideas from everyone in writing and only then shares that with the whole group. And, if you want to further prevent group dynamics from influencing the process, then distribute the collected information and ideas *anonymously* the first time.

3. **Play the devil's advocate:** To ensure all arguments are challenged and seen from multiple perspectives, it can be useful to empower someone to ask challenging questions. These are the critical or opposing questions that no one feels comfortable asking because they may upset those who argue *for* a specific position. But by *appointing* someone to the role, that person gets the *right* to challenge—and thus, it shouldn't feel so upsetting to those whose ideas or viewpoints get contested. This technique is called playing the "devil's advocate." And if everyone in the group knows the concept, you can use it when you feel the need for a counterargument to be heard. Then you can say, "Let me play the devil's advocate for a moment," and then follow that with a counterargument or challenging question.

4. **Deliberately ask quiet group members for their input:** To make sure that everyone is heard, you can actively ask the quieter members of the group to contribute their opinions. Especially in meetings where outspoken people tend to dominate, the more silent may not get enough opportunities to contribute. But by *actively* involving them, their ideas and opinions can be taken into account. You don't have to be the group leader to include the quieter group members; everyone can take responsibility for that.

5. **Call for a time-out:** If negative group dynamics hinder the decision-making process, you can suggest a time-out. Then the situation can be revisited, and maybe some changes can be made to move forward in a more constructive way.

6. **Split the group:** Sometimes a group needs to develop a wide range of ideas and think outside of the box. Then it needs to use as divergent thinking as possible and tap all the creativity it can—and avoid narrowing in on one or a few ideas too early. One way to facilitate that is by splitting the group into two or more subgroups that each is tasked with—for example—generating alternatives or thinking about pros and cons. Then, when the subgroups are finished, they gather again and share their work, which is almost guaranteed to include more divergent thinking than if they had worked in one big group.

SKILL 11

NETWORKING

- Networking is about personal connection.

- Build your network long before you need it.

- Seek out new people to gain new perspectives.

Almost everything you accomplish at work involves other people. They are, of course, often your colleagues but can just as well be people outside your own team or organization. And the more and closer relationships you have, the better the chances that someone you know will have the knowledge, resource, influence, or contact you need to accomplish a particular task or goal. Likewise, the better the chances that *you* can help someone else in your network. Helping each other out is the essence of what networking is about—because then *everybody* has access to a bigger pool of knowledge, resources, and connections.

Don't underestimate the value of building a network. You'll have to invest time and effort in it, but it'll be an investment that pays handsome dividends. Because as your career progresses, your network will become more and more important. Remember the distinction between important versus urgent? Networking is one of those activities that really *is* important—while rarely urgent. Don't be too busy or focused on short-term results to skip it. Instead, think of networking as an ongoing, daily activity.

Like any other professional skill, networking can be learned. It is not reserved for people who are especially outgoing or talented in interacting with others. Anyone can do it while acknowledging their personal style and strengths. There is no one-size-fits-all to networking; you can follow your own unique way and do what works best for *you*.

But before we dive in, let's get the definition clear. Fundamentally, networking is about *personal* connection—relationships that you build and nurture with other people, one person at a time or as part of working together in small groups. It's about basic human interaction that everybody enjoys and benefits from. It's not about posting on social media or collecting friends, followers, or connections; while being engaged on social media can supplement your networking activities, it cannot replace personal connection. Building a network must also be for the *right reason*: to build mutually beneficial relationships for the future. Thus, you build your network long before you need anything from it. Networking is about "paying it forward"—without expecting or asking for anything in return. You *give* value to someone in one form at one time and *receive* value from someone else in another form at another time.

Why Is a Network Important?

So, what are the benefits of having a network? More than you might think. First, a strong network makes you more effective in your job; it makes it easier to get things done quickly and efficiently. A strong network equals influence, and that influence may be as valuable as formal authority and power. Especially the network and relationships you have *internally* in your organization are essential for influencing things and pushing things through. When you need to draw on special skills or knowledge, your network gives you someone to reach out to, or someone to ask if *they* have someone in *their* networks with the special skill or resource you're trying to locate. For instance, if you need to contact someone in another organization but don't know who the right individual is, it helps if you know a person there who can guide and refer you.

Your network also helps you develop professionally and personally. If you build a diverse network, you get access to a whole range of different ways of seeing and doing things, which will broaden your perspective and help cultivate your understanding of other people's situations. A broad network within your organization also lets you see how everything fits together and how people and processes depend on each other. Knowing people in different teams or departments allows you to contact them and ask them professional questions or ask them to teach you something.

And, as discussed in Skill 4: Building Resilience, your network can help support you when you hit setbacks. When things are difficult and you're frustrated, it's invaluable to be able to reach out to others and get advice or a comforting word; to be brought back to reality if you've lost perspective; or, maybe, to just laugh at it all with someone you trust.

Finally, a large proportion of job positions are filled by candidates found in people's networks. For example, if you dream of working in another part of your organization, your chances of hearing about or being considered for an open position are much higher if you know some people there.

In sum, your network can be essential for your career and well-being. It gives you influence, makes you more effective at what you do, develops you, makes you more resilient, and helps you find new and exciting opportunities. And, hopefully, many of your connections become friends or at least trusted and valued relationships that you enjoy spending time with—people who give meaning and purpose to your life.

Think of Your Network as Concentric Circles

You'll likely interact with thousands of people throughout your career. That's many more than you'll have time to actively keep in contact with, even if you wanted to. Thus, you need to make some choices. You cannot invest equal time and attention in all of them; you have to prioritize. To aid in that, it helps to think about your network as three concentric circles: your inner, middle, and outer circles.

In your *inner circle* are the people most important to you. They are those you invest the most time in to keep the relationship going. They are those you *actively* do something to keep in touch with (if you wouldn't otherwise be in contact)—for example, by having a coffee or a meal together, keeping in touch by chat, phone, etc.

Your inner circle includes people you know well, genuinely like, trust, and enjoy spending time with (professionally or otherwise). If these basic criteria aren't present, they cannot be part of your inner circle—at least not in the long term. Because it will never feel sincere and authentic.

With people in your inner circle, you are—mutually—on each other's minds. You help each other without hesitation if you're asked, and you proactively do things for each other. For instance, when a professional opportunity or interesting job pops up, you think about each other and maybe reach out and inform the other person about it. The same goes if you meet someone you believe would be of interest to a person in your inner circle, then you introduce them to each other.

In your *middle circle* are people you have spent enough time with to think of them as your network—albeit not as your *inner* circle. You have observed enough of each other's behavior and performance to have established some degree of trust and respect. That may be as colleagues or as parties in commercial transactions, such as supplier, customer, consultant, client, partner, etc.

Because the basic test of mutual respect has been passed, you'll both probably respond to requests and be willing to help each other out, at least in some limited way. You may spend a bit of effort from time to time to "ping" each other—for example, by congratulating each other on birthdays, commenting on social media, occasionally sharing something interesting, etc.

In your *outer circle* are all the people you don't have the current capacity, or interest in, to actively stay in touch with. They may be people you've worked with previously, people you've met at professional events, or people who have contacted you for professional reasons. Or perhaps people you've only recently met and exchanged contact information with for future use, but nothing more.

While you've met (physically or via phone, video, etc.) and know who each other are, you'll probably not do much more to *actively* stay in touch. Again, because that's just not practically possible.

However, that doesn't necessarily matter, as the value of the relationships in your outer circle lies in the fact that you *have* met and *do* know each other, at least superficially. And that makes for a big difference to complete strangers. Because if you need to reach out to them, you're not reaching out to a *stranger* but to someone you already know. That's the value of your outer circle: you can reach out to them, even after years of no contact. And they can reach out to you.

For example, if someone you once knew now works in an organization you want to get in touch with, you may reach out for tips and advice. If you have a relevant question or business proposition, it's perfectly okay to contact someone you only met casually, even years ago. For instance, you could reach out like this: "We met at the A conference three years ago, and I still remember our conversation about B. I'm now working on B and wondered if I could ask you . . ." If you made a good impression when you met, you'll likely get a positive response, provided that your ask is appropriate and makes sense.

In your outer circle, there's really no limit to how many connections you can have because you don't spend time actively managing them. You may do something to stay on people's radar by posting, sharing, and commenting on things online, but you don't spend much time actively staying in touch on a person-to-person basis. That way, your outer-circle connections may be counted in many hundreds or even thousands after years in your career. Note, however, that your outer circle does not contain people you have *never* met or interacted with. For example, if you connect with a stranger on LinkedIn, that connection has very low value before you've had some kind of personal interaction. Thus, that connection is not part of your outer circle yet—it's just a digital link.

Summing up, if you think of your network as concentric circles, you won't get overwhelmed by actively maintaining too many connections. Instead, you can invest most of your time in your most valuable relationships: your inner circle. When you meet *new* people, you can connect with them (for example, on LinkedIn) and keep each other as contacts for the future. And nothing more is needed; you don't have to spend effort maintaining the connection (because that's now stored in LinkedIn). If you find the relationship valuable, you can start keeping in touch on a more regular basis and thus develop your new relationship into a closer connection. In the same way, some of the people in your inner and middle circles will fade out with time. Thus, who's in what circle will be ever-changing as you (and the people around you) change jobs, locations, and industries as your careers develop.

LinkedIn

You'll likely use many different platforms and social media apps to stay in contact with your network—Facebook, Twitter, Instagram, email, text messages, WhatsApp, etc.—but one platform in particular stands out for professional networking: LinkedIn.

LinkedIn is important because it's focused solely on *professional* networking. It also has an enormous user base: more than 800 million at the time of writing. That means that the dominant part of the working population will be on LinkedIn in many countries. (If LinkedIn is not available or significant in your country, find out which other platform is and apply the following practices to that.) Because LinkedIn is used by so many, it makes a lot of people visible to you who would otherwise be much harder to find.

LinkedIn has a host of features, but this book will not go into detail about them. However, what's important is not that you understand and use all these features, but that you have actually signed up with LinkedIn, created a presentable profile, and started using it. Because while you *can* (of course) network without LinkedIn, it's just much easier when you use it. If you're not on LinkedIn, it may raise the question "Why not?" as it is simply expected in many professions. Even if you're still a student while reading this book, you can start using LinkedIn now. And you probably should, if you've got less than a year left of your education.

Your LinkedIn Profile

The first impression anyone gets of you on LinkedIn is the top visible part, which can be seen without scrolling. That is your name, photo, headline, summary, and background photo. These elements must immediately give a positive and professional impression. Your picture is important, so make sure to upload a current and high-quality photo of yourself, clothed appropriately for your job (or your dream job). That's not a selfie, by the way. Choose a descriptive headline and write a short summary about who you are and what you stand for. You can also mention some of your best accomplishments. While many people don't use this feature, you can upload an appropriate background photo, like one related to your industry or the organization you work for.

Next, the sections describing your education and job experience must also be filled in with accurate data. For each job and education entry, best practice is to write some sentences or bullets that detail what you did and what you accomplished.

There are many additional sections you can fill in, such as skills, courses, languages, awards, certifications, and publications. You don't have to fill in all these sections, but it's good practice to fill in the relevant ones to give people a better understanding of who you are. This additional information also helps you to be found when people search for a particular skill or experience on LinkedIn. For example, when a recruiter is searching for a certain keyword, it *has to* be part of your profile for you to be found.

In any case, don't gild or prettify your profile; that can make you appear as self-important or untrustworthy. The purpose is to give truthful information that credibly communicates your background. Also, familiarize yourself with the latest LinkedIn changes and best practices, and take inspiration from how other people make their profiles.

Finally, get someone to review your profile—also for grammar and spelling. And keep your profile updated, including your photo and contact information, which should always be current.

Using LinkedIn

When you've met someone and want to connect on LinkedIn, it's simple to reach out. Just look them up and send an invitation, but make sure to *personalize* it. For example, "Hi, Mark! It was great speaking to you yesterday! I would really like to stay in touch in the future. Best, Peter." It doesn't have to be a long message, but it should be a customized message and not the default; that's much more personal and shows that you care. Once you're connected on LinkedIn, you can now use the messaging function to stay in contact in the future (or use some other means of communicating).

Another useful functionality is posting things (updates, articles, etc.) on LinkedIn. Many people don't use this function, but, like with any other social media platform, it can be a great way to increase your visibility. With LinkedIn, however, your posts have to be strictly *professional*. This is not the place to share inappropriately personal stories, pictures, or videos. And certainly not for sharing political or social views.

Who Should You Network With?

If you haven't already, the simplest way to start your network is to begin with the people you *already* know well: the colleagues you're working with and other relevant people in your organization. In most organizations, it's only natural that people connect (typically on LinkedIn) as they get to know each other. Next, it's family and friends, and also the friends of your family and friends—if you know them well enough. Also, people from your social network like schoolmates, neighbors, and other people from sports activities, volunteer work, clubs, etc., as long as you think they're relevant to your network and you like and trust them.

You should also build professional relationships *outside* of your own organization. They can be anyone you meet as part of your job, as long as it makes sense. It might be business partners and acquaintances from other organizations or people you meet at events, seminars, and conferences. If the relationship is professionally relevant or you like the person, why not connect? You can simply think of them as new additions to your outer circle, which allows you to find each other again—even years later—if something pops up that makes it relevant. If you take this approach and keep connecting with people outside of your usual circles, you'll find yourself with a diverse network of people from many different professions, industries, countries, cultures, ages, etc. And that is an extremely valuable asset!

Regardless of where you meet your new connections, don't hold back from connecting with people who have very *different* opinions, lifestyles, natural strengths, and experiences from yourself. Often, the people who are different from yourself are the ones you can learn the most from. So don't shy away from people who are complementary to yourself (people who have strengths where you have weaknesses).

Finally, you can reach out to strangers, people you have never met or interacted with before. But you should only do that if you have a concrete and professionally relevant reason. For example, if the other person is an expert in a domain and you believe that you might build a relationship of real value for both of you. Networking has to have a purpose. You don't just add people to your network to make it *larger*.

Add Value

As you reach out to others, you may wonder, "What's in it for *them*?" While you understand the value for yourself in building a network, you may feel uncertain about what kind of value *you* can bring to the relationships you build. You might think that you're too inexperienced to have much value to offer. However, there are more ways to add value than you might think. Below is a list that you can use as inspiration and reassurance that you actually *do* have value to offer. Even small things you only spend a few minutes on may be of considerable value for the other person.

- **Providing information:** One of the most common ways to add value is by providing information. That may be on your own initiative if you see something you believe is interesting for a person in your network. Or obviously, if someone asks directly for it. Examples are books, websites, articles, blogs, pictures—any kind of helpful information.

- **Things that you're proficient in:** As most of your colleagues are often older than you, there are many ways you can add value because you are *younger*. For example, you have access to the newest knowledge and theory. And you likely understand technology, social media, and the digital space better than many of your older colleagues. Here is a big area for you to add value.

- **Connecting people:** Your own network can be valuable to others, as it's *your* unique network—consisting of, for example, peers from your education. That means that if someone needs a piece of information or to talk with someone who possesses a specialist skill that you don't have yourself, you may be able to connect them with someone (from your network) with the right knowledge. Or, you might, on your own initiative, introduce people to each other if you believe they would benefit from connecting.

- **Giving advice and bouncing ideas:** Often, just being available for discussion, bouncing ideas, or providing feedback and advice is all the value other people need—and highly appreciate. Especially if you tell the truth as you see it and don't sugarcoat things. Simply being a sounding board for someone else can be very helpful.

- **Providing information about job openings:** If you hear about an open position—in your own organization or elsewhere—you can inform the people in your network who might be a good fit for it.

- **Listen and empathize:** You can also provide value by simply listening and giving support when others in your network are under pressure or frustrated (professionally or in their personal lives). Then providing support, advice, understanding, compassion—or whatever the situation calls for—might be exactly what they need the most.

If Networking Feels Uncomfortable

At least for some people, one difficulty with networking is that they feel uncomfortable when they reach out to people they don't know well and start a conversation or ask to connect on LinkedIn. Because reaching out can be associated with fear of being rejected. Consequently, networking may bring about one's insecurities and self-doubt; you may ask yourself, "Am I smart/good enough?" or "Will this person like me?" However, keeping with the *same* group of people all the time isn't good either. That limits the professional and personal development you get from interacting with a variety of people and deprives you of the value you can get from a broad network.

But how do you overcome yourself and reach out when you feel uncomfortable about it?

First, as stated in Skill 3: Building Confidence, you have to start *doing* the activities you want to build confidence in. So start small and gradually build confidence in networking by training yourself to reach out to people and adding them to your network. Make it a habit.

Second, remind yourself that you're not asking to be best friends, only to be professionally connected. Networking is simply part of being professional; it's an everyday practice. You're just making relevant connections, which is, in fact, a productive part of your job. And most people appreciate it when someone makes the effort to reach out.

Deliberately Seek Out New People

To expand your network beyond those you usually work with, you have to make a little extra effort. You may have to break out of your comfort zone now and then. But it's worth it; there's *so* much value in getting to know people who are different from the ones you usually associate with!

At your workplace, the best way to do that is to be *deliberate* about seeking out new people and relationships. Especially if you have a habit of hanging around with the same people most of the time, you need to break out of it. For example, at lunch, at the coffee machine, at company events, try—at least sometimes—to seek out new people to be with and talk to. Sit at another table, go to another coffee machine, stand at a new place. Be open and curious and try to connect in ways that fit the situation, whether that's talking about work, the weather, sports, telling jokes, or whatever you feel comfortable with.

Also, when you happen to work with someone from another department or team, take a little time to get to know each other; don't just move on to your next task as soon as your work interactions are finished. Let's say, for instance, that you work in IT and meet someone from logistics as part of a project. Then it's perfectly okay to introduce yourself with a few more details about you personally and then ask the other person about his or her job. You can also say that you're new and want to learn and understand what's going on in logistics. With a positive attitude, your request will very likely be well received. And soon, you'll be on your way to a new connection that might, over time, turn into an inner-circle relationship.

Connecting with others in your organization also includes connecting with people both up and down in the hierarchy. Let's assume that you've been to some meetings with a manager a level or two above you, who you would like to connect with, and you believe that you've made a positive impression. Then it's fine to invite him or her to your LinkedIn network (or whatever means of networking you prefer). *You* can take the initiative; you don't have to wait for the higher-ranking person to invite you first. Of course, connecting with powerful and influential people can feel uncomfortable. But do it anyway if you believe it makes sense; you'll often be pleasantly surprised at the response.

Outside of your workplace, it's the same thing: to expand your network, you need to deliberately interact with *new* people. That is, for example, when you take part in conferences, training courses, networking events, business meals, and social events. Even if it feels awkward, try to strike up conversations with new people—most are courteous and friendly. Just be straightforward and casual; don't make it a bigger deal than it is. And if there's a good connection and conversation, that's just great. However, if the other person doesn't seem interested, don't worry about it; simply move on to another person. No one can be a good match for every person they meet. Also, don't spend your time on your phone or laptop; when you want to meet new people, you need to look approachable and open.

Finally, it can be useful to do some planning. When you arrive at a new workplace, you can be systematic about who you want to get to know. Make a plan for who you want to meet and write it down. Get some input from your manager or experienced colleagues about who they think would be good for you to know. That could, for example, be people in your organization who are good contacts for your job role or have the same specialist skills as you. Or maybe people with the same job function as you, but who work in other workplaces. Then deliberately try to meet and get to know these people, one by one.

Follow Up within 24 Hours

When you want to connect with new people you've just met, you should follow up soon after while your meeting is still fresh in your minds. Best practice is to be in touch within 24 hours. For example, if you've met someone at a conference and would like to stay in contact in the future, send a personalized LinkedIn invitation the same or next day. Again, a little extra effort to make it personal goes a long way—for example, by referring to where you met or what you talked about. That personal touch makes it much nicer for the other person to receive your invitation.

If you can include some kind of value at the same time, that's even better. For example, some information, a relevant link, a name, or an invitation to an event. Or you can simply offer to continue your conversation if you had something valuable going on.

Reaching Out to People You Don't Know

Sometimes, you want to reach out to specific people for professional reasons. Maybe because they're just good at what they do, and you want them to be in your network. Or perhaps because you believe you can do business together in the future. Here are some ways you can go about it.

One option is to try to *meet in person* somehow. For example, if you know that someone you want to meet is coming to a meeting, a company event, or a conference, you can search for him or her and try to get together. You can also join the same interest groups and communities as the kinds of people you want to connect with and then get to meet them that way.

Another good way is to use someone in your current network as *a reference.* If the person you're seeking knows someone in your network, you have someone in common you can use as a reference. LinkedIn is very effective in finding that out because you can see all the connections of all the people *you* are connected with. That can be a lot of people who are just one person away from you! Maybe the individual you're looking for is one of them. So check out LinkedIn (or other social media sites) and see if you have someone in common. Before you reach out, ask the person you want to use as a reference if it's okay and makes sense. If your reference doesn't know the other person that well—or for some other reason doesn't want to be a reference—then using your contact's name wouldn't be appropriate.

Alternatively, if your common contact knows both of you well, he or she may be happy to *introduce you* to each other. That's an excellent way to make contact when possible. The introduction can, of course, be done in person, by email, in a video call, etc.

Finally, you can reach out via email, phone, Twitter, LinkedIn connection request, or some other means. This is sometimes referred to as a "cold call," as the other person doesn't know you. When you make contact, make a personal and well-considered request that explains who you are and why you want to get in touch. If you can refer to a common professional interest or something else you have in common (e.g., an education or a former workplace), that also helps.

SKILL 12

GETTING AND APPLYING INFLUENCE

- Influence is earned, not given.
- Take the initiative.
- Understand "what's in it for them."

To get things done, influence is often necessary—either in the form of something you *have* (where influence is a noun: you *have* influence) or something you *do* (where influence is a verb: you *apply* influence).

When you *have* influence (the first form), people will automatically listen to you and take you seriously. You won't have to prove yourself first; they already know who you are and believe in your skills and competence. The first part of this chapter will show you two ways to get influence: by building a well-earned reputation, and by taking responsibility for the bigger picture.

When you *apply* influence (the second form), influence is something you *do*. It is an act where you actively apply influence to change a specific situation or obtain a specific outcome. In the second part of the chapter, we'll go through two ways of applying influence: by taking the initiative, and by using influencing techniques.

Note that all behaviors and techniques presented here are productive and appropriate. None of the negative behaviors that people sometimes associate with influence or politics are needed; no manipulating or dishonest behaviors are necessary (or desired). In fact, one of the best ways to gain influence is to build a reputation as being *unpolitical* and straight-talking. That earns you trust and, hence, influence.

Luckily, most organizations' cultures are predominantly good and honest: people succeed without negative or deceptive behaviors. Of course, you *will* sometimes experience improper political tactics. That's hard to completely avoid. But if you find yourself in a *predominantly* toxic culture, you might want to consider if you're in the right organization—or, at least, in the right part of that organization.

Build a Well-Earned Reputation

Many of the skills introduced so far are strongly linked to influence. Think about it: Wouldn't you say that someone who has great professional behaviors, is a team player, has a good working relationship with his or her manager, and is competent, effective, and trustworthy might be someone who is taken seriously and listened to? Absolutely. That naturally translates into a well-earned reputation and gives influence.

So, to get influence, you always need to build a track record of solid performance. You don't just *get* influence; influence is *earned.* And the foundation it stands on is your proven ability to create value. There is no influence without having first proved yourself. Most jobs have a learning curve in the sense that you need to get actual experience with key tasks and responsibilities before you'll be seen as competent.

That means that you—in any job—always start with focusing on doing the job you're hired to do very well. You start with proving that you can deliver the value you're expected to deliver, and that includes *soft* skills like behaving and communicating professionally, being a proper team player, working well with your manager, making sensible decisions, and so on. Together with your hard skills, that's your foundation for influence. If you start initiating things and try to exert influence without having first built that foundation, you may just create noise and frustration. So have a little patience and build your well-earned reputation first.

Take Responsibility for the Bigger Picture

If your scope of work is narrow, your scope of influence will be narrow. If your scope of work is broad, you can make things happen on a larger scale, and therefore, your scope of influence will be broad.

Consequently, an important element of influence is to look beyond one's own job and focus outward, on the larger picture: the team, the organization, the clients or customers, and the industry. As you better understand how *your* work contributes to the whole, you can better improve it and work more effectively. And you can take ownership of results outside of what you yourself produce (e.g., customer satisfaction, patient well-being, or product quality).

So, as you gain experience and confidence, it's time to lift your vision outward. That also goes hand in hand with broadening your network. You shouldn't focus solely on *your own* job and priorities, but be curious and broaden your scope of interest to other or larger parts of your organization. To do that, ask (lots of) questions and research the workplace and culture you're in. Try to understand, step-by-step, how it all fits together.

The first point to focus on—beyond your own job—is your team. Try to understand the roles of everybody in your team, the value they're creating, and how it adds up to your team's total contribution. Talk with your peers and your manager and ask them to explain your team's overall goals and how *your* work contributes to those goals. And when you get new tasks and assignments, ask for the meaning behind them and the larger picture they're a part of.

Next, turn your attention to the department, division, or other relevant parts of your organization. Whenever you have a chance to work with people outside of your own team, grab that opportunity to learn about what *they* are doing and what *their* objectives are. To get a more cross-functional understanding, you can also ask your manager to help arrange practical experiences in other departments or job functions. There is no better way of understanding how others work than spending some days or weeks actually working in their environment. Suppose you are an engineer. In that case, some practical experience at a construction site or production unit will undoubtedly be very instructive and could extend your network with some new people you would otherwise not meet.

Also, explore how your organization is structured. An excellent place to start is the organization chart. Most organizations have up-to-date organization charts and directories with all their employees. Those charts and directories are a perfect way to get an overview and are very useful for looking up people's names and jobs when you cannot remember them. Your organization's intranet is usually also a great source of all kinds of knowledge, such as history, projects, systems, processes, strategies, success stories, newsletters, and learning portals with a wealth of training you can take (at least in bigger organizations). Use these assets to educate yourself. Try to see all the way through to the needs and wants of those your organization ultimately serves, such as customers, clients, patients, guests, consumers, students, etc. That also helps you get a better perspective of the value *you* are contributing in *your* job.

Finally, research your industry. If you know the trends, players, technologies, current challenges, etc., you can participate in many more discussions at a qualified level. To get input, look around in your organization and ask your colleagues—there's likely lots of relevant information. But also do your own research: read industry publications and blogs, attend industry events, and take additional training to stay up to date.

If you're ambitious, there is one more thing you can consider: If you don't already understand financial statements and budgets, you may want to educate yourself. Because, in *any* type of organization, money governs. At the end of the day, money is one of the essential languages of management. Every decision has financial implications, and understanding them is necessary to get initiatives and decisions approved. So (at least some) understanding of finances and budgeting processes will be beneficial if you participate in any form of decision-making.

Take the Initiative

It's necessary that you see your job as both *accepting* tasks as well as *initiating* them. If you perceive your job as solely accepting instructions and assume a position of waiting for the next thing to do, you're missing half of the equation. Because you shouldn't just do what you are *asked*. In most jobs, it's also your job to *take the initiative* and seize opportunities and anticipate problems and events—and not just wait for others to do it. As an intelligent and independently thinking team member, it's your job to assume responsibility. For instance, if you run out of productive work, you don't just passively wait for someone to give you your next task—you proactively seek it out, either by initiating your next thing yourself or asking what to do next.

The wait-and-see approach also has an unfortunate long-term consequence: you don't *train* yourself in taking the initiative. Because, like any other skill, the skill of proactively initiating things has to be trained and kept in shape. If you make it a habit to wait for others, you actually train yourself in the opposite: to *cede* responsibility, initiative, and control to others. So avoid this trap. While it—in the short term—may feel comfortable waiting for others to take the initiative, this habit will slowly weaken your own capacity to initiate things.

Of course, taking the initiative can be risky, as your initiative may turn out to be a bad idea or be met with resistance. Thus, taking the initiative may require you to take a risk and move beyond your comfort zone. On the other hand, if nobody initiates anything, nothing happens; organizations *need* initiatives and innovation to stay vital and develop. And everybody should feel responsible. That's why most managers highly appreciate it when people in their teams can work independently and initiate action themselves. It frees up the manager from a lot of work and draws on the skills and creativity of the whole team instead of only the manager. It's much more effective when everybody is proactive and contributes initiative—and not just the managers.

Obviously, when you take the initiative, your ideas *will* sometimes be turned down. And sometimes your initiatives *will* turn out to be a mistake. But still, on average, those who initiate change and take action are far more valuable and influential than those who don't. So don't be afraid to make yourself visible with the initiatives you take; it's a necessary and value-adding behavior. Good intentions alone don't change anything.

But how do you actually *take* the initiative? Below are four ways. Use them with situational judgment, as cultures and managers differ; some managers are very good at delegating and ceding control, while others have a strong need to be in control themselves. And the latter type may not like you showing too much initiative. Or, at least, they will want to be very well informed.

1. **Ask.** If you need something or want to initiate a change, you have to *ask*. The idiom "It never hurts to ask" is usually true. The worst that can happen from asking is you get turned down—and then you're no worse off than before. You may fear that worse things *could* happen—that you would offend or stand out negatively by asking— but that's unlikely if your ask is well thought out and justified. So be willing to ask, even if your ask is bold. The best way to ask is to be straightforward and not make it complicated. Ask with an *expectation* of getting a yes—that will make you more self-confident and it will shine through in the way you ask. If you don't get an immediate yes, listen for what flavor of no you're getting. Maybe it isn't a definitive rejection but an opening to get a yes if some things are adjusted. Or perhaps it is a "no, not *now*," which opens up for asking again when the timing is better. Importantly, don't be offended or take it personally if you get a clear "no." Move on and spend your energy on something else.

2. **Set the agenda.** When some work or activity has to be done, the best way to influence things is to take the initiative. For instance, you can propose or volunteer to be the person who makes the preparation, sets the agenda, writes the report, prepares the draft, organizes the people, develops the plan—or whatever has to be done. The person who creates the work, especially at the beginning of a new initiative, has enormous influence on the content. And as other people are often busy with *their* stuff, they are usually quite happy to let somebody

who steps forward do the job. This is one of the easiest ways to apply influence: simply propose that *you* do the work. However, be careful that you are not just pushing your own interests and needs while not considering the positions of others. That will likely give pushback, and you risk losing support. Most results are created by *teams* of people, so—as a good team player—remember to continually align with other relevant people.

3.   **Seize the moment.** Sometimes opportunities for influence appear quite suddenly, and then you have to seize the moment. Such moments usually don't last long, and the opportunity may soon have gone again if you don't act. Those moments often require that you make a quick decision because you don't have the luxury of ample time to think things through and weigh the pros and cons. So you have to take the risk. An example of such a moment can be when a colleague is suddenly unavailable, and someone has to take his or her place; when some crisis or emergency arises; or when someone unexpectedly has to participate in a special meeting, a job interview, or a negotiation. Such opportunities are also good openings to try out new things, meet new people, and widen your network. Note that as well as seizing such moments for *yourself*, you can also grab them on behalf of *others*—let others have a shot at the opportunity. That builds friends, trust, and collaboration.

4.   **Seek out the right team.** If you want to be in a more influential position, you usually have to actively do something to make it happen. For example, suppose you're working well in your current job but feel that you don't have the right kind of influence. Or enough influence. Then you can take the initiative to change things: seek out another team, project, or part of the organization where you can have more influence. Work with your manager—or other managers—to effect the changes you want. Because if you don't actively do something yourself, it's much less likely to happen. But also have a bit of patience with your current job, as it *does* take time to get influence.

Influencing Techniques

Most jobs require you to sometimes actively apply influence—often without having any formal authority. For example, when you have a specific task, project, or product that you need to promote, or if you have an idea for a business opportunity, a process improvement, or something you believe should be changed or stopped. In these cases, you can significantly increase your probability of a successful outcome if you use a few influencing techniques.

Simplifying things, you can think of applying influence as three steps: 1) preparing, 2) pitching, and 3) persisting. The rest of this chapter will walk you through each of these steps.

Step One: Preparing

The very best way to win over other people is to understand them. If you want them to do anything, you need them to want to do it *themselves*. You cannot force anyone to have an opinion or want something; you can only try to help them convince themselves. And the way to do that is to understand what's in it for them. So you need to turn your full attention to the needs and wants of those you want to win over. If you understand their motives and needs, you can much better make a pitch that relevantly speaks to them. Basically, you need *empathy* to influence others.

Unfortunately, that's where many influencing efforts sadly go wrong from the beginning: because those who try to exert influence focus too much on themselves and the idea or product they are promoting and not enough on "what's in it for them." Consequently, many sales and idea pitches miss the target right from the beginning. They miss what's important for *the receiver* of their messages. So, you have to put yourself in *their* shoes and ask yourself, "What's the benefit for them?" and "Why would they be interested?" In fact, the best pitches don't often focus on the product or idea at all—they focus on the *needs* of those you try to convince.

Understand the Value for Them

Part of "what's in it for them" is understanding the ultimate value of what you're promoting. Many people make an elementary error with this: mistaking ideas, projects, or products for value. Because they are not *value*; they are merely *means* to create the value that an organization really seeks. Value is what those you try to win over will *gain* if your product, service, or idea actually works.

Value can often be interpreted in financial terms like cost, inventory, productivity, sales, etc. Or in nonfinancial metrics, such as return rates (in retail), medication errors (in health care), on-time rates (in transportation), customer satisfaction, employee turnover, time savings, and quality (in all organizations). Since metrics like these are the language of decision-makers, *you* often need to also think in these terms when you prepare a case. Let's say you need to promote the idea of investing in a new machine, piece of software, tool, or similar asset for your organization. Then you should not only present its *features*—like speed, usability, efficiency, design, precision—but also the *value*. For instance, that might be lower costs or time savings. With some well-argued and educated guesses on the value, decision-makers can compare the cost of your proposed investment to the value it will provide. And they can compare it to other investments. Preparing yourself this way can make it much easier to get a case approved.

So, while features and properties are important and obviously have to be presented, you also need to understand the ultimate value. If you find that difficult, work with your experienced colleagues or your manager to understand the impact of the idea or project. They can probably help you express it in terms of value.

Understand Their Self-Interests (if Any)

Sometimes people think not only in terms of the value for the organization but also in terms of the value for *themselves*. So if anyone you're trying to win over has a self-interest in some way, you need to understand it. Consider what needs, challenges, ambitions, and goals *they* personally have that your idea or project might help them with. That may be things like recognition, influence, status, power, resources, or publicity. Likewise, if the proposal is somehow working against such interests, people might fight it instead—even if the proposal really is in the overall interest of their organization. Therefore, you have to always consider people's self-interests. They may weigh heavily on their position for or against your proposal.

Understand the Decision-Making Processes

Another part of your preparation is to understand *how* decisions of the kind you're seeking are made. It's a common mistake to underestimate the timings and formalities of decisions. Even if you've gained support for an idea from colleagues and other people, that may just be the beginning of a longer journey, as those supporting you may not have the necessary influence or decision-making capacity.

If the idea is somewhat complex or has a non-negligible cost, it often needs to be presented to and approved by many people, more than you might expect. Even relatively small decisions may have to be approved by your manager's manager or higher. And many decisions have to be approved by other functions—for instance, finance, quality, legal, purchasing, HR, security, etc. The formal decision-making processes may require that a number of these stakeholders are in agreement or informed. And that takes time and effort. So if you don't know these processes and requirements, you need to understand them or work with someone who does.

Plan Your Meetings and Conversations

Before you start pitching an idea or project, you need to plan who to speak with and in what order. Of course, sometimes a "sell" *can* happen in one step, and if that can be done, by all means, seize the opportunity. If it isn't complicated, don't make it!

Often, however, it's not as simple as that, and you'll need to talk with multiple people or groups. If that's the case, be methodical; think about your "campaign" as one step at a time—one conversation, one email, one presentation, and one meeting at a time. Articulate for yourself what your objective is for each meeting and conversation. Because if you don't know your goal, how can you go for it? For example, in some meetings, you may just want to introduce your idea and get feedback and advice. In other meetings, you may look for support or for resources, or to build alliances. And in yet other meetings, you may be seeking decisions.

Step Two: Pitching

Okay, now you're finally in a meeting or on the phone with some important stakeholders. What's the best way to go about it? How do you make your pitch?

First, the communication principles from Skill 6: Communication apply. You may want to reread the section about "common principles." In particular, the principle "Adapt to the style of the receiver" is critical. *Adapting* your message to each person or group you meet can be key to gaining support. Therefore, before you meet, consider what kind of language and arguments best speak to them. For example, some people prefer rational arguments backed by facts and data. They like to see hard evidence and logic to assess an idea. Other people are more convinced by a vision and a passionate approach. If they can envision an idea and its purpose, they may decide based on that—and not so much on the hard facts (even though they'll probably still want to see them).

Another aspect of "adapting to the style of the receiver" is how technically proficient the audience is. A common error is presenting an idea or a project in too technical detail and using too technical terms. Especially when you're an expert in what you present—and your audience is not—it's easy to assume that they understand your topic as well as you do. But that's usually the wrong assumption. So you need to adapt your message to your audience's level of expertise. Otherwise, all they hear may be technical "blah, blah, blah" that's not convincing anyone. Note that adapting is also something you should do *during* a conversation or presentation. If you feel that the other part isn't getting it or is drifting away, you need to adjust your message and not hammer away with what you have planned. You have to be flexible and shift your approach based on the reactions you get.

In addition, a number of other principles are helpful when pitching to others. This book is not about sales techniques or making presentations, but the below eight principles will take you a long way in making an impact in meetings and one-on-one conversations. For more detail, go to other sources—for instance, an in-depth book about sales or presentation techniques.

1. **Start by establishing rapport.** Unless you already know the individuals you're pitching to, you always want to start with spending a few minutes establishing a connection and a good atmosphere. That shows your genuine interest and that you don't just consider them means to accomplish a goal. Have a little chat or small talk, professional or personal, before diving into matters.

2. **Keep it simple.** If you're deep into your idea or project, you probably want to explain a lot of details and arguments. But that might just overwhelm your audience and water down your *main* points with too much information. So choose only the best and most relevant arguments for the person or group you speak with. You don't have to give them everything you have; if they want *more* information or in-depth explanations, you can give them that *later*. But if you start by giving them too much, you may flood them with more information than they can digest. Keeping it simple also counters the temptation to present weak arguments. Because you, in most cases, should never have to present any weak or flawed arguments. A shorter list, consisting of only strong arguments, is much more convincing.

3. **Impress from the beginning.** You want to grab the attention of your audience right from the start. Especially busy people usually grow impatient with an elaborate approach that only reaches a conclusion after a long speech. Consequently, you typically want to *begin* with your conclusion and best arguments. Then you're off to a good start.

4. **Use examples, stories, or demonstrations.** Most people connect much better with tangible rather than abstract content: something that affects their emotions, like a concrete story with real people having real problems. Or something they can see or touch, like a demonstration, a mockup, or a prototype. Therefore, to the extent you can, try to include such elements in meetings or conversations. People will almost always remember a story, an example, a demonstration, or a prototype better than abstract concepts and explanations.

5. **Don't be unduly biased for your own case.** If you're so eager to present the merits of your idea or project that you forget (or deliberately omit) its drawbacks, you risk coming across as untrustworthy or deceptive. You cannot act as if disadvantages or obstacles don't exist if they do. And if the person or group you're trying to convince starts seeing you as biased or insincere, no amount of arguing the merits will help you. Trust and credibility come first. Therefore, it's better to present not only benefits but also drawbacks. By presenting the disadvantages (which your audience probably already knows or will find out anyway), you can preemptively address them. By doing so, you come across as more credible and with a stronger case.

6. **Ask questions.** When you promote your case in a conversation or meeting, it shouldn't be one-way communication. Don't be so preoccupied with explaining your case that you forget to connect with your audience. Rather, you need to *ask questions* to clarify if your case actually fits the needs and wants of the other side. You need to understand "what's in it for them," and asking questions is the shortest way to that. Listen well to the answers—not only to what is directly said, but also for any *underlying* needs that they are indirectly expressing.

7. **Handle objections like catching a ball.** Imagine that a ball is thrown at you. What do you do—try to catch it? Or try to avoid it? You need

to handle objections like the first option: *catch* the ball. Trying to avoid objections by brushing them off, minimizing, or ignoring them will be a red flag for those you're trying to convince. Instead, take it positively. An objection is, in fact, often a sign that the other party is interested in what you're saying and is now testing it to understand its limits. Thus, an objection is an opportunity to understand what's on the other person's mind. Frequently, you can reply with "Thank you, that's a good question / a valid point" and elegantly catch the ball like that. Then, like any feedback, you need to *understand* the objection. Listen closely, ask clarifying questions, and explore it until you understand it. Now when you have constructively received the objection, you can respond. If you don't know a good answer to the objection right away, admit it and don't try to hide it. Promise to return with a response later. That just adds to your credibility.

8. **Let your enthusiasm drive you.** Real, heartfelt enthusiasm is a powerful force. When you work with something you genuinely care about, that will energize everything you do, including when you talk about it. Thus, let your conviction and passion for your case shine through and carry your message. Enthusiasm is contagious, so if *you* are convinced about what you say, other people will also be more easily convinced.

Observing the above principles, you are now well into a successful meeting, but how do you *close* it so that some progress is actually made? Basically, if the other side isn't by themselves proposing to do what you want, *you have to ask*. This is the moment that sometimes makes people nervous because they fear getting a "no." And that fear holds them back from asking. But asking for what you want is necessary.

If you believe that what you want may be too much to ask for *from the beginning*, you can instead ask for a *smaller* next step that's still valuable but less committing. That may be easier to get acceptance for than a big commitment. Such a step-by-step approach toward your ultimate goal often has a higher probability of succeeding. For example, some next steps could be:

- Permission to work more with the idea and maybe spend some resources

- Permission to present your idea to someone else, possibly higher up in your organization

- Permission to access some experts to work with you on the idea

- Permission to make a small-scale experiment, test, or pilot project

Proceeding in smaller steps also makes sense because it reduces the risk decision-makers must take. And that makes it easier for them to give a yes. You can, of course, go for a big and bold ask, but be ready to present a plan B with a more modest next step in case you get a no.

Step Three: Persisting

To fully implement something can take considerable time. It often requires someone to actively and persistently drive things on a day-to-day, person-to-person basis. Therefore, the last step in applying influence is to *keep going* until you get the commitments, actions, and results you need. You have to be persistent; to keep pushing to keep the momentum going. Basically, the job of applying influence isn't over when you get a yes. It's over when the idea or project is *a reality*.

So you need to follow up and see your idea or project all the way through to the end to be sure that it succeeds (or hand it over to someone who does). For example, if someone promises to do something—add to a budget, talk with someone, do some work—you often need to follow up to make sure it actually happens. That's the kind of "push" you have to maintain to ensure that things stay in motion and eventually get implemented in a meaningful way.

AFTERWORD

It isn't easy to master all the 12 universal skills, but the closer you come, the more fulfilling a work life you'll have. Not only will *you* have a more rewarding career, but you'll also contribute to making more harmonious *workplaces*. That translates into better results created by happier people with less stress and frustration. We know these are big words, but that's how critical these skills really are! So use them to make the most of your potential, inspire others, and make a positive impact. We know you can.

Review Request

Social proof through reviews is critical to building relevance for all products, including books. We believe this book can make a positive difference in many lives, but it is *your* view that counts. So, we have a small ask: Now that you have finished reading the book, we would be grateful if you could post an honest review. Your candid review can help others decide whether this book can improve *their* chances of thriving and succeeding in their careers.

To make a review, you only need to go to the review section on the book's Amazon page. There you'll see a button that says, "Write a customer review" – click that, and you are ready to go! It's a similar process on other online bookstores or book review sites like Goodreads if you prefer to leave your review there.

Thanks,
Nina & Peter

APPENDIX

JOB SEARCH

Like any other skill in this book, job search can be learned. And with your knowledge about the 12 universal skills, you're in an excellent position to go job hunting. Note that job search here refers to both *internal* and *external* search; most of the steps are just as applicable for searching for jobs internally in your organization as externally.

The first step on the path to a job is to realize that job search takes time and effort. Of course, you may get lucky and get your dream job quickly, but most of us don't have that kind of luck. Securing a job is too important to be something you let depend on *luck*.

Below are twenty-four concrete how-to steps that will be hugely helpful. They are presented in the natural order you need them. You don't necessarily need to do all of them.

Step 1: Organize Your Job Search

Before starting, set goals for your job search—for example, applying for five jobs a week or speaking with two new people every week who can inspire and guide you. And set up a system to organize your search so you don't miss or forget anything. Use a spreadsheet to keep track of applications you have made, people you have contacted, interview dates, correspondence, and people to be contacted in the future.

Additionally, make a folder for every job you apply for where you save a copy of the job posting, your research, cover letter, résumé, and other relevant documents.

Step 2: Check Your Public Profile

As recruiters will likely search your name, you need to ensure they get a decent first impression when they find you on LinkedIn, Facebook, Twitter, etc. Beer drinking and unprofessional profile pictures shouldn't be the first thing they see.

A good way to check your public profile is to run an incognito search for yourself on Google or another search engine. Review everything you find, also back in time. Then take down any posts or pictures that aren't appropriate for job search. If others have posted something that reflects poorly on you, ask them to take it down. You may also want to change the privacy settings to better control what others see as public content.

This is also the time to ensure that your LinkedIn profile is in good shape, as described in Skill 11: Networking. Note that for job search purposes, you need to take extra care to include essential keywords.

Finally, you need to check that your email address works for professional purposes. Preferably, it should just contain your name. A funny email address you invented when you were eleven isn't giving the right signals or could be outright ridiculous. So, if needed, get another email address to use in your job search.

Step 3: Always Research Organizations You Apply To

Few things are as off-putting to recruiters as applicants who clearly don't know much about their organization. They immediately risk being perceived as "résumé-sprayers" who just send their résumés around and hope for the best. But they're not likely to get many positive reactions with that approach, because it's crucial to *customize* everything to the specific job and organization you want to work for. And to do that, you need to research your potential new workplace.

You need to research both the job role *and* the organization, such as its products or services, mission, history, values, culture, locations, etc. Remember to pay special attention to the culture; you want it to fit *your* style and *your* values. Look at the organization's website, LinkedIn page, social media, press coverage, annual reports—whatever makes sense. Contact those in your network working in the same workplace or in similar roles in other organizations and get tips and information. And if the organization sells physical products, try them out, watch some videos, and check some reviews.

If you've done thorough research, it will show in your cover letter and in interviews and show your seriousness. You obviously cannot know everything, but a solid, basic knowledge of the organization where you may soon be working is a must.

Step 4: Engage Your Network

Many jobs are never advertised, as employers can often get enough applicants from referrals and unsolicited applications. Consequently, your network can be key to your job search. Remember the recommendation to start building your network *before* you need it? This is one of the reasons why.

To engage your network in your job search, you must inform them that you're looking for a job so they can start staying alert for relevant opportunities. If they don't know that you're looking for a job, they can't help you. Especially if you're looking for your first job, it's helpful to let as many people as possible know that your search has begun. But don't just tell them that you're looking for *a* job; be much more specific and tell them what types of jobs you're looking for, in which industries, etc. That makes it easier for them to help you.

You can also try to get "informational meetings"—an informal conversation with someone in the industry, organization, or job role you're targeting. Your objective should be to get *information* or *inspiration*, not necessarily a job in *that* organization. In fact, *don't* ask for a job—most people won't be able to give you one and will thus be reluctant to engage. Instead, when you frame your request as purely seeking information or inspiration, more doors will open for you. To get informational meetings, ask yourself who in your network works in the industry you want to work in; in a specific organization you would like to work for; or who might know someone who does. Then contact them—in person or in writing—and tell them you're looking for a job and what types of jobs, and that you would like to have a chat. Ask them for tips, advice, skills you need, relevant contacts—any kind of information that can help you in your search.

One way to find relevant people to network with and have informational meetings with is to use the LinkedIn *alumni* search function, which allows you to see everyone who has studied at the same educational institution as you. This functionality is super useful to discover the right people to contact. Besides, having shared the same school experience gives you a nice way to introduce yourself.

Step 5: Apply Unsolicitedly

Applying unsolicitedly for jobs is often surprisingly successful, especially with small- and medium-size organizations where the distance between you and relevant managers is relatively short. If you make enough unsolicited applications (of good quality), there's a good likelihood that some of them will be received by someone who has a current or upcoming need. With a bit of luck, the receiver is considering opening a new position, or an employee has recently left or resigned. That's your unique chance if the job hasn't yet been publicly advertised. If you're a fitting candidate for the job, then the hiring organization will save time and money by hiring you instead of going through the standard recruiting process. Applying unsolicitedly for jobs may feel more uncomfortable than seeking publicly advertised jobs, but that's part of the success of this method: the initiative and confidence you show with an unsolicited application already speaks in your favor.

Before you apply, you need to research the organization you want to work for, as described in Step 3. Recognizing that you obviously cannot know what kind of positions might be open, you should still do your best to tailor your application to the organization you target.

One approach is to apply *personally*—typically by phone. You can reach out to specific managers if you have their contact information and a good reason.

Otherwise, you can contact HR. Don't worry if you don't get the right person on your first attempt; just ask *who* the best person is for you to talk with. Have your customized sales pitch ready in front of you when you call. Your goal should be to get a meeting or interview. Initially, though, the best outcome you may hope for is that you're asked to send more information—and that's good because now you have a dialogue going.

Applying by email is also good and may be the better option in large organizations. Follow the cover letter guidelines in Step 12 (adjusted to the fact that you are applying unsolicitedly) and attach your customized résumé.

Finally, many organizations also invite unsolicited applications on their websites (usually where current open positions are listed). If you use this channel, follow the instructions for applying.

Step 6: Look Broadly for Advertised Jobs

Besides looking for jobs via networking activities and unsolicited applications, you can obviously apply for advertised positions.

When you look, be sure to look broadly. Jobs are advertised in many different places, and no employer uses all of them. If a hiring organization can get sufficient qualified candidates by advertising in only a few channels, they will do that. Consequently, if you look too narrowly, you may be missing relevant opportunities. For example, most organizations post their jobs on job banks. But they may prefer some job banks over others. So, to see all the relevant positions, use all the job banks where the types of jobs you're looking for might be posted. You can also create a profile and upload your résumé to job banks. That way, you make yourself searchable.

Job/career fairs are another great way of meeting organizations looking to hire fresh graduates or trainees. To get the most out of the career fairs, come prepared. Research the organizations you're most interested in—you don't want to start your conversations with "So, what are you doing?" And don't target only the most well-known brands, as you may have your best chances with the lesser known. You could be one of only a few people talking with them rather than one of many.

Otherwise, open positions can be found on hiring organizations' websites, LinkedIn, newspapers, and professional associations' websites and magazines.

Step 7: Closely Read the Job Posting before You Apply

The key to writing a good application and making a good impression in the interview is to really understand the information in the job posting. You don't want to overestimate, nor underestimate, the expectations. Or misread anything. So you need to read the job posting closely and repeatedly. This practice also avoids wasting your (and the hiring organization's) time applying for jobs you're not qualified for or that don't fit you. Here are some tips on how you should read job postings:

- **Look for keywords.** Identify important keywords in the text and highlight them. They are the qualifications the employer is looking for.

- **Look for repetition.** The skills, knowledge, and characteristics mentioned more than once across the job posting are most important to the employer.

- **Notice the ordering of bullet points.** Responsibilities and qualifications are often listed as bullet points, and the order they're presented in usually indicates the order of preference. The most important items are generally listed at the top, and the items at the bottom may be "nice to have" but not actually required (even if that's not explicitly written).

Now, having read the job posting carefully, you must decide whether to apply. Remind yourself that it's common to explore and experiment at the beginning of your career (you may want to reread Skill 2: Setting Goals at this point). So, don't be fixated on finding the *perfect* job. Instead, be flexible and open—also to opportunities that may not be your first choice.

Additionally, it's important to understand that the job posting may not be particularly accurate. It isn't easy to write a good job posting, and the result can be that the job content is communicated vaguely or with too many "nice-to-haves" that aren't realistic to find in a single person. So don't skip applying for a job just because you don't check every single box. Find the confidence to go for it—even if it seems more expansive than you feel you can handle. Often the requirements aren't as difficult as you might fear. Or you may get some training and be up to speed quicker than you expected.

On the other hand, you *must* meet the majority of the highest prioritized requirements as you understand them from your close reading. Not necessarily *all* of them—and certainly not all of the "nice-to-haves." But the top of the most important requirements—yes.

If you believe you meet enough requirements, then ask yourself three questions. Do you think you would actually be happy with these responsibilities? Do you think you would fit with the organization's culture and values? And do you think this job fits what you want in your career at this stage? These questions are essential because it's just as important that the job matches *your* expectations as it is that you match *the hiring organization's* expectations. So do a gut check before you spend time applying.

Step 8: Select Relevant References in Advance

Employers will usually ask you to provide two or three references at some point in the hiring process. And as they may put a lot of weight on what references say, you want to select the best ones you can find.

Typically, references are past managers or colleagues. The best are past managers who speak positively about you; that's enormously helpful. But if you're seeking your first job and have not yet had a manager, then past teachers, coaches, and volunteer coordinators are just as good.

So consider who would be the best references for you, then contact them in advance and ask for their permission to use them as your reference. Ask if they feel comfortable being a reference for you—you want to be sure they'll speak positively about you. If you get a lukewarm answer to that question, don't use them—you need references who are predominantly positive about you. It's okay if they know some of your weaknesses (nobody is perfect), but, in general, they need to be people who would recommend you.

Remember to get permission from those who agree to be a reference to give out their contact information. And ask them how they would prefer to be contacted. In addition, provide them with your résumé and tell them what job—or jobs—you're applying for.

Step 9: Build Experience Where You Lack It

Employers often want to hire people with experience. But how do you get that experience if employers won't hire you because you lack experience? Many new graduates encounter this paradoxical problem when searching for their first job. The solution is to *build* that real-world experience.

Here are three suggestions:

An internship is obviously a great way if you can get one, even if unpaid or only modestly paid. Internships may be available in all kinds of organizations, big and small, government, private business, and nonprofit. You can find some internships posted on company websites and job banks. You may also apply unsolicitedly to the organizations you're interested in. Or use an internship office or a specialized internship finder service.

Another way is through volunteer work, typically in nonprofit organizations or community activities. These organizations have lots of work they need to get done by volunteers, and if that fits with the skills you need to gain experience, then go for it. Experience gained from volunteer work can be just as valuable as if that experience was gained through paid work.

You can also get creative and *create* the opportunities you need to gain experience. For example, if you need experience building social media presence for a professional organization, why not contact small local companies and offer to do a free project for them (or to do it for a small sum)? That's a win for both of you. It's up to you to take the initiative: you provide value—for free or for a modest pay—and the organization, in return, gives you the experience you need. You just have to get creative and take the initiative to make it happen.

Step 10: First, Make a *Generic* Résumé

Having a high-quality résumé increases your chances of passing the first, crucial selection step where only the most relevant résumés are passed on to the interview rounds.

First, you need to make a *generic* résumé that *generally* fits the type of job you want. This version should have all your relevant job-related skills. This is the one you'll upload to job banks. And it's also your base from which you later create the *customized* versions you use when you apply for specific jobs (Step 11).

Note that the term "résumé" here refers to a short (one or two pages) document. In many countries, the term "CV" (Curriculum Vitae) is used for the same thing. However, in the US, the term CV refers explicitly to a comprehensive document, with no length restriction, covering all relevant academic and professional achievements. It's typically used for applying for certain academic jobs, but that's not the topic here.

Before you start making your résumé, make two steps of preparation.

First, make a brain dump of *all* your skills and experiences. This is the raw material from which you create your résumé. Ask yourself: What are you good at—and what makes you good at it? What do others think you're good at—and why? If you lack professional work experience, think broadly: include any experience you've gained from other (possibly nonpaid) sources. That might be internships, sports, volunteer work, community activities, student council work, coaching others, relevant coursework and projects, hobbies, exchange programs, and even gap-year experiences. When you look broadly, you *will* find experiences that are transferable to what employers are looking for. Experience, especially for first-time job seekers, doesn't have to be *paid* experience. What counts is that you have a history demonstrating that you have the right skills and can maintain a job.

The second step of preparation is to get an overview of which qualifications the type of job you seek typically require. A great way to do that is to copy and paste the text from five to ten relevant job postings into a word cloud generator or text analyzer that finds the frequencies of words (these tools can be found for free on the internet). The word cloud or frequency counts will give you strong hints about which skills (both hard and soft) you should include in your generic résumé. These keywords are important because they are what recruiters and automated HR systems will be scanning for in the first phase of the candidate screening.

Having prepared yourself this way, you're now ready to write your generic résumé. It shouldn't be overly creatively or cleverly formatted (unless you're applying for a creative job). That could make it harder to read—both for humans and systems. Since recruiters may only spend seconds with your résumé, you want to make sure the information is quick and easy to find. So, it's usually best to use a standard template with a generic and predictable look. There are thousands to be found on the internet; choose one that's appropriate for your industry and the type of job you're applying for.

The typical résumé includes these sections:

- **Summary:** Also called a professional or executive summary. In this short section, you write a few lines that, in essence, are a sales pitch of why *you* are a good fit for *this job*. It should answer why you're qualified for the position and how you'll add value to the organization. To make it fit in the short space, you need to prioritize—only the most important information can go here. Note that it is *not* a summary of your work history, etc. That can be read elsewhere in your résumé.

- **Experience:** A condensed description of your relevant experience, listed in reverse-chronological order. Write what your responsibilities were and what you accomplished in those roles. Note again that if you have little or no professional experience, you can include unpaid and volunteer work here.

- **Skills:** You can write both hard and soft skills, often as two individual subsections. Use your knowledge from this book to list your strongest soft skills.

- **Education:** List them in reverse-chronological order.

- **Personal information:** Your address, telephone number, email address, and a link to your LinkedIn profile. If you live far from the workplace, indicate that you're ready to relocate.

- **Other sections:** Include other relevant sections like certificates, licenses, interests, languages, courses, personal projects, or hobbies.

- **Relevant links:** You can also include relevant links. For example, to your online portfolio (in creative industries) or to your personal blog (if you're a subject-matter expert or writer).

Put yourself in the recruiter's shoes when you write the different sections. Think about it: If you were a recruiter who received hundreds of résumés from applicants all claiming to be "results-oriented," a "self-starter," or a "high performer," would that make any of them stand out? No, such buzzwords would just sound hollow. Vague claims like these are useless for recruiters unless they're backed up with accomplishments that prove the points. So, for instance, if you say that you're "results-oriented," then be sure to include examples of results you have achieved to back up your claim.

You also want to make your résumé easy to understand for people who don't have your background; you cannot assume that the person reading your résumé has the specialty knowledge you have, or know the organizations you've previously worked for. Therefore, it's helpful to write a sentence or two about the size and industry of each of the organizations you've worked for. Do the same with your education: write a few sentences or bullet points about what it covers, including what you've specialized in.

Finally, get your résumé reviewed by at least three people, preferably with relevant experience and background. Some of them should also know you well. If you don't get feedback on your résumé, you likely have a *big* problem. Because you *cannot* see its flaws. So take this step seriously—don't skip the feedback. It will take additional time, but it makes your résumé much better. You can also buy online services to get feedback where professional recruiters help you optimize your résumé.

As a final check, make sure your résumé has perfect spelling and grammar. You don't want it to stand out negatively because of grammar or spelling mistakes. That's a red flag for recruiters.

Step 11: *Customize* Your Generic Résumé to the Actual Job

With your generic résumé created, you're ready to apply for *specific* jobs. But you should never send your generic résumé with your application. Instead, you need to *customize* it to the specific aspects of the job you seek: the industry, the organization, and the job position. You want to build a compelling résumé that closely aligns with what the employer seeks. The sole purpose of it is to land you an interview.

Based on the job posting and your research, you can now customize your generic résumé to the actual job you're applying for:

- *Remove* qualifications that are not relevant to the particular job you're applying for. They're just taking up space and distracting the reader from what's important.

- *Add* qualifications from the job posting that are not in your generic résumé. Analyze the job posting to find out if there are essential qualifications that don't appear on your résumé but that you have. If you actually have that skill, knowledge, or experience, you need to add it (make sure it's spelled the same way). Of course, only add a qualification if you actually have it—don't stretch the truth.

- *Add* unwritten qualifications. Often, job postings don't mention *all* requirements. Therefore, you can also include skills and experience you *know* are relevant but just aren't mentioned.

- *Customize* the summary section with a text that clearly articulates how you fit the particular role and organization and how you'll provide value. Your research will be helpful here.

- *Optimize* for the most essential qualifications. Both humans and systems will put more weight on the qualifications that appear most frequently on your résumé. So try to fit the top most important keywords from the job posting into your résumé in two or three places (not only once). For example, you might include them in the summary, experience, and education sections.

- *Add* two or three references if asked for by the employer.

Note that some job banks allow you to automatically use the résumé you've already uploaded when you apply for jobs. But don't do that; you want to *always* customize your résumé.

Step 12: Write a *Customized* Cover Letter

A cover letter is a means to introduce yourself and entice the recruiter to think, "Wow, we really need to interview this candidate!" So your cover letter cannot sound generic like it's being used over and over again for different positions. Instead, like your résumé, you must tailor it to each job you seek. You may obviously reuse some of the content, but most of the text usually needs to be adapted.

JOB SEARCH | 215

Remember the pitching principles "Keep it simple" and "Impress from the beginning" from Skill 12: Getting and Applying Influence? They're also vital when writing cover letters. Keep your cover letter simple by making it short and super relevant—no fluff. No more than three hundred words. If it's longer, you risk recruiters skipping it or only reading the first few lines. And impress from the beginning by showing your very best assets and arguments right from the introductory paragraph. Then you hook the reader to read the rest.

While a cover letter is formal and often follows a standard structure, your *language* doesn't have to be formal. Quite the opposite; if you can write it in a simple, everyday language, that just makes you shine through more as a person. And that's difficult to convey in the résumé, which is a more fact-based format. One way to ensure it sounds right is to read it aloud, then you can quickly hear if anything sounds overly formal or unnatural.

There are, of course, innumerable ways to write a cover letter. And there's no single best way to do it. But there are also many ways to get it wrong, so it's best to follow some kind of proven standard. Like with résumés, there are many templates you can grab on the internet, which is probably a better idea than beginning from scratch. In any case, below is a great structure for your cover letter. If you follow that, you're off to a good start. Keep all paragraphs at a maximum of three to five sentences, and make sure the most important keywords from the job posting appear one, two, or three times.

- **Header:** Name and title of the hiring manager (if you know it or can find out) and name and address of the recruiting organization. Your name, phone number, and email address. And, optionally, your title, home address (or just your hometown), and link to your LinkedIn profile.

- **Greeting:** Start with a salutation you're comfortable using. If you know or can find out the hiring manager's name, then address the cover letter directly to him or her. For example, "Dear Mr. Flores." Otherwise, use a generic greeting like "Dear Hiring Manager" or "Dear X Team."

- **Introduction:** The opening paragraph should immediately grab positive attention and entice the reader to read on—you want to show your value right from the first sentence. You can emphasize a few of your concrete skills or achievements that are highly relevant to this job, or you can express why you're particularly enthusiastic about *this* job or organization. Note that the first sentence must mention which job you're applying for.

- **Your qualifications:** In this paragraph, write the highlights of your qualifications, including selected skills (hard and soft), experience, and accomplishments. This is basically telling the organization why they should hire you. The paragraph should answer the question: What value will you bring to the table if they hire you?

- **Your motivation:** Building on the previous paragraph, explain why this job is an excellent fit for you—professionally and personally. This paragraph should answer the question: How and why is this job such a good opportunity for me?

- **Closing:** In one or two sentences, tell the hiring manager that you welcome the opportunity to meet in person and discuss how you can be of value to the organization. If relevant, you can also mention that you would be interested in other positions in their organization.

Finally, read your cover letter over multiple times and thoroughly check for grammar and spelling.

Step 13: Follow the Instructions When You Apply

After all your hard work, you want to avoid making a technical slip when you send, upload, or type in your application and other information. Therefore, closely follow the instructions indicated in the job posting. You don't want to be passed over due to a formality.

If you're asked to apply via an automated HR system, then have all the elements of your application ready in front of you. And have patience; some of these systems take time to navigate. Use the requested file format if you upload your application online (usually PDF or Word). If you're unsure, use PDF. And use a standard font—HR systems might not read fancy fonts.

Step 14: Follow Up on Your Application if You Don't Hear Back

If you don't hear back from the hiring organization, it's usually perfectly okay to follow up. But don't be too quick to do so; you have to give the employer reasonable time to process the applications they receive (that's typically at least a week). And take a look at the job posting first; it may ask applicants to refrain from following up or state a specific response date. In those cases, you shouldn't follow up.

If you have the contact information, it's best to call or email the hiring manager. In fact, that only shows your dedication and sincere interest in the job. When you call or write, be brief, humble, and polite. Just ask where they are in the process and reiterate your genuine interest in the job. You can also add one or two quick facts about yourself and why *you* are a terrific fit for the job. But not more.

Step 15: Prepare for Tests

Cognitive ability tests, sometimes called intelligence tests, are standard in many organizations when candidates are selected for the interview rounds. Before the interview, the candidates are asked to do different tests, either on-site or online. The tests measure the candidate's mental skills like reading comprehension, critical thinking, numerical reasoning, etc. And while you cannot change your intelligence, you *can* effect your test scores by familiarizing yourself with how they work. Also, try to practice some of them under the same time constraints. You can find sample tests on the internet.

You might also be asked to take a personality or strengths test, such as Myers-Briggs, DiSC, or CliftonStrengths. These tests are used to help recruiters understand how the candidate's preferences and natural strengths fit the role. For example, the best matching strengths for a salesperson and a software tester could be quite different. You shouldn't fear these tests. Just answer them honestly; there are no right or wrong answers. To familiarize yourself with how they work, you may want to try some out for yourself before encountering them when seeking jobs. Various tests can be found on the internet, usually for a reasonable fee.

Step 16: Create a Story Bank

Real stories make a pitch much more engaging and memorable. Use this approach in your interviews: talk about *specific situations* to make what you say more credible.

However, when you're under pressure, good stories usually don't conveniently pop up in your mind just when you need them. Therefore, prepare them in advance: create a *story bank* where you store your best (and professionally relevant) stories so you can remember and practice them. Then they'll be much easier to recall when you need them. The way to do that is to take time to recall experiences related to the type of job you're searching for. Specifically, you need stories that can be used to exemplify typical interview questions.

For example, try to remember situations where you . . .

- made an outstanding achievement; something you were proud of
- demonstrated initiative
- overcame challenges and solved problems
- were a team player
- made a mistake, but fixed it and/or learned from it
- had to give critical feedback, and it went well
- received critical feedback and learned from it
- worked with a difficult person and handled it well

For each of these situations, *write down* your stories. Be specific; include some details, struggles you went through, etc., as they make your story come alive. Your stories shouldn't be long, just relevant. And they should, preferably, be about recent experiences—not something you did ten or fifteen years ago.

Step 17: Practice Answering 10 Common Interview Questions

With your story bank made, you can prepare for some typical interview questions. This is important, as it prepares you for questions you hadn't seen coming and thus risk answering in unfortunate ways. The following are ten typical questions you will encounter, plus tips for answering them. You can look up more interview question examples on the internet.

1.   **Tell me a bit about yourself.** This is often the first question. It allows the interviewers to catch up and orient themselves to who they're talking to. The best way to answer it is by following the same formula as for writing your cover letter: (1) introduction, (2) your qualifications, and (3) your motivation. You should *not* answer this question by rambling on about your entire life story; that's not what the interviewers are after. Instead, make it short and focused on the professional requirements of the job. They can always ask for more details if they want.

2.   **What was your greatest achievement [in job X]?** The interviewer wants to know some of your successes from your previous work history (or school or youth jobs, if you're a fresh graduate). Use relevant stories from your story bank for this question.

3.   **Tell me about a big mistake you've made.** The interviewer is testing your self-awareness and honesty, so if you cannot come up with a mistake or a failure, that's a red flag. Everybody makes mistakes, including you. The way to answer this question is to have one or two stories ready that honestly describe a real mistake you've made and how you corrected it and/or learned from it.

4. **What are your greatest strengths?** This question is directed more at generic strengths and soft skills like communication, strategic thinking, analytical skills, and attention to detail than at hard skills. Don't be too humble when answering this: mention one or two of your truly best strengths that are especially relevant for this job. And remember to exemplify them with stories from your story bank; don't use vague buzzwords or phrases that are not supported by a real story.

5. **What are your greatest weaknesses?** Like the question about mistakes, be honest and talk about real weaknesses. We all have strong and not-so-strong sides—and admitting to a few of your weaker sides isn't a negative but just shows that you're authentic and have self-awareness. For instance, maybe you aren't comfortable with public speaking. Of course, you don't want to detail a long list of weaknesses, but honestly talking about a few of them won't hurt you. Just don't pick weaknesses that may hamper your ability to do the job you're applying for. The key to turning this conversation into something positive is to *also* talk about how you *address* your weaknesses. Again, be prepared with examples.

6. **Why did you apply for this job / Why do you want to work here?** Interviewers ask this question to understand why you're interested in working in *this* exact position for *their* exact organization. If you convince them that you're genuinely enthusiastic about working there, they know you'll do a better job and are more likely to stick around for the long term. So you want to clearly convey you want *this* job—and not just *any* job. You need to tell them two things: (1) why your qualifications are a perfect match for the job and what value you will contribute, and (2) why you are enthusiastic about this particular job. The key to answering this question is to express your genuine enjoyment of completing the tasks you'll be doing in this job, using concrete examples. You also want to talk about what you find particularly attractive about this organization: their products or services, their reputation, their culture, that you'll be working with talented people, etc. Whatever it is, you should talk about it with genuine enthusiasm.

7. **Why do you want to change jobs / Why did you leave your previous job?** If this is not your first job, you may be asked this question. The answer depends on why you're leaving: either (1) because you're currently employed and seeking a better opportunity or (2) because you left your job on your own accord or were fired. In the first case, you should talk about what you want to get *to* instead of what you want to get *away from*. For example, if you're bored in your current job or feel that there are too few interesting challenges, you could say: "I want more ownership; I'm ready for bigger challenges." But don't say: "I'm bored." In the second case—if you were fired or quit—it's best to have come to terms with what happened and calmly explain it in a few sentences. Keep it simple and talk like a professional about it. Don't start attacking anyone or act like a victim. Most people have tried to be fired, and they know it can happen—for many reasons. And in all cases, never talk bad about your previous workplace or manager. It's better to be neutral or positive; for example, you can say: "I enjoyed my years at [organization X], met some amazing people, and I learned a lot, but now I am ready for . . ." That's much better.

8. **Where do you see yourself in five years / in the future?** As noted in Skill 2: Setting Goals, setting detailed goals five years out in time is difficult and may not even be meaningful (especially at the beginning of your career). And the interviewer knows that. So there's no need to be super specific with your answer—and it's not expected. However, your response should lie within the domain of what your new employer does. If you answer, for example, something in an unrelated industry or that you want to be an entrepreneur, they know that your long-term aspirations are not in *their* organization. Therefore, good answers fall within career paths that fit your new organization, such as taking on bigger projects and responsibilities, being a subject-matter expert, learning the industry in and out, etc. You can also add to your answer by turning the question around and asking what your new role's growth paths are.

9. **Why should we hire you?** Your answer should convey the value that you bring to your new workplace. You shouldn't talk about yourself and what a great person you are, but (in line with the pitching principles) see it from *their* point of view. And what the employer wants is value for the salary they pay you. So tell them, using specific examples, how you will address the challenges of the job and create value if you're hired. Tell them how *your* skills, knowledge, and experience are an excellent match for those challenges.

10. **Do you have any questions for us?** Usually, this is the last question. What's important is that you actually *have* some questions ready for the interviewers. If you don't really have anything you want to know more about, you could appear uninterested. And that's the last message you want to send! So prepare some questions before the interview. Which questions you should ask obviously depend on who is in the interview: if it's the hiring manager, you can ask detailed questions about the role and its challenges and responsibilities, the team, the strategy, etc. And if it's a recruiter or an HR representative, you can ask more high-level questions—for example, about culture and the next steps in the hiring process.

If you've made your story bank and prepared answers to those ten common interview questions, you're likely much better prepared than most other applicants. But to be as prepared as possible, you still need to *practice*. Remember from Skill 3: Building Confidence that you build confidence by *doing*? It's the same with the interview questions. Therefore, ask a trusted friend, a family member, or a career advisor to practice with you. Or perhaps, practice by yourself by speaking out loud in front of a mirror or by recording yourself.

Step 18: Exhibit Your Best Professional Behaviors

You obviously want to exhibit professional behaviors at the interview (as detailed in Skill 5: Professional Behaviors). Make sure you dress appropriately for the occasion, are at least fifteen minutes early, and turn your phone off as soon as you've announced your arrival. Exhibiting your best professional behaviors should be something you do throughout *all* stages of the hiring process: in telephone and video calls, in emails, in the lobby, and in interviews. You treat everyone with the same professionalism and respect.

Also, be equally well prepared for telephone or video interviews as if they were in-person interviews. Ensure that you select an environment conducive to a professional conversation: no distractions or noise, and never when you're driving or walking. For video interviews, ensure you're dressed just like you would be for a physical interview and sit in tidy surroundings with proper lighting.

Step 19: Exhibit Your Best Communication Skills

Giving the other person your full attention, being an active listener, smiling, maintaining eye contact, and keeping an erect and confident posture all weigh heavily on how you come through in the interview (see also Skill 6: Communication). That's important right from the beginning of the interview: the *first* impression interviewers get of you has a lot of influence on how they finally evaluate you.

Therefore, if it's a physical interview, stand up tall and take some deep breaths before entering the building. It'll give you good posture. Keep the posture throughout your whole visit to come across as confident—even if you don't feel that way inside. When you meet the interviewers, give them a firm and assured handshake.

Also, be mindful that a job interview is not meant to be a one-way conversation only. Do your best to make it a two-way conversation: you can also ask *them* questions (actually, you should) and take part in exchanges about professional topics as an equal. Remember, you're there so the interviewer can get to know you, and the best way to do that is by engaging in real conversations. Put yourself in the interviewer's position: If you were interviewing a candidate who primarily answered with short sentences of a few words and then kept quiet, how could you get to know that person? So, when appropriate, try to turn questions into conversations. That makes you more human to the people interviewing you and allows the conversation to better show who you are and how you talk and act in everyday situations.

Step 20: Let the Interviewer Get to Know You

Before the interview, it's good to refamiliarize yourself with your research, the job posting, and your résumé and cover letter. Also, rehearse your story bank and answers to the ten common interview questions.

If you know their names, then research the hiring manager and others who you know will interview you. Search for them on LinkedIn and other social media and check out their profiles and activity. This exercise will likely make them seem more human and help you better connect with them.

When the interview starts, then—in general—let the interviewer lead the conversation. While you should aim for two-way conversations, it's still the interviewer who has the lead. Be prepared to talk through your résumé, even though the interviewer can read the same information directly in it (it's a good tip to bring a printed version of your résumé for yourself). Take your time to answer the questions you're asked, and don't worry if you don't get to say everything you have in mind.

Also, be yourself. It's just as important to you as it is to them that you fit the role and team. Consequently, you need to stay true to yourself. For instance, if you don't function well with conflicts and the interviewer keeps on coming back to how you handle conflicts, it's okay to turn the table and ask, "Are there current problems with conflicts in the team?"

The same goes for your qualifications: If you try to give the impression that you "can do everything," you may come across as untrustworthy. Because *everybody* has their preferences—their strengths as well as weaknesses. So it's better to be transparent. That also shows you have self-awareness. For example, it's okay to say, "I am really good at A and B. I have little experience in C, but I'm a quick learner, so that shouldn't be a problem. And while I can do D, it's not my strongest skill, so I wouldn't want that to be my main task." When you're honest, like in this example, interviewers know they can trust you. Plus, if skill D isn't essential for the role, then it doesn't matter that it isn't one of your strengths.

You can also differentiate yourself by mentioning something about you that is *unusual* and makes you memorable. Think about it: after interviewing, maybe, a dozen people stretched over several weeks, it can be difficult for the interviewers to remember who is whom. Try to give them something special to remember *you* on. For instance, if you're really good at some sport or activity, or have a unique hobby. Then you can make yourself stand out as the "geocaching guy" or the "judo woman." A hint to this should also be mentioned in your résumé.

Finally, if you feel that the interviewer forgets to ask you important questions, you may need to sell yourself a little more. Try to find ways to talk about your key qualifications, even if the interviewer doesn't touch on them. There isn't much to lose by trying to effect how the interview goes if you feel that your most relevant skills and achievements aren't getting told.

Step 21: Follow Up after the Interview

If you still want the job after the interview, then, within 24 hours after the interview, send an email to those who interviewed you thanking them for the opportunity and restating that you're interested in the position. This will keep you top of mind for the interviewers and show that you're eager to get the job. It's also what many employers expect: If you *don't* send a follow-up email, they might interpret that as a lack of interest. So do it.

As with every other communication in your application process, customize your email; make it personal for the receiver. Refer to a specific topic discussed in the interview and how *your* skills and experience will help create value for your new employer. But keep it brief: just a few highly relevant facts.

Step 22: Consider the Whole Package, Not Just the Salary

Your salary and benefits package are *not* something you should bring up during your first interview. If you do that, you risk giving off the impression that you're not sufficiently interested in the job and mostly thinking about what's in it for you.

Instead, wait for the employer to bring it up, which typically happens in the second interview. In fact, waiting to bring it up just gives you a better negotiating position: because by the time *they* bring it up, they're likely very interested in you. So it doesn't harm to be patient; quite the contrary. And before you get into a dialogue about compensation, research the typical salary range for the type of role you're applying for.

Then, don't focus on salary alone. A job is so much more than the salary: the job being meaningful, how much responsibility you have, your colleagues, the organization's values, your manager, opportunities for mentoring, prospects for an exciting career path, the commute from home, development and learning programs, flexible scheduling, opportunities for remote work, paid phone, healthcare plan, pension scheme, bonuses, vacation days, wellness programs, etc. Therefore, take the *whole* package into consideration. If you cannot get the exact salary you're hoping for, you might be able to make up for it with some of the other parameters that are valuable to you.

When it comes to the negotiation, it's generally best if you can get the employer to go first and mention what salary and package they have in mind for you. You might be surprised that it's better than expected. If they ask you directly to say first what *you* have in mind, then try to initially avoid mentioning any numbers but say that you are open and would like to understand the full package that they propose. However, if there's no way around it, then cite the research you've made and place your proposal in the middle or upper half of the range that your research suggests is fair. Emphasize any special skills and experience you have that may justify that. Don't mention the absolute minimum you would accept—you can always fall back to that later. Then, finish the negotiation by focusing not only on the salary but also on the other parameters of the package.

Finally, when you're offered the job, read the contract before signing and, if possible, get someone else to read it who knows your field of work.

Step 23: Respond Constructively to Rejections

Despite your best efforts, getting rejections is part of the process. Remember, job searching is a probabilities game: if ten candidates interview for a job, nine of them will get a rejection. If three candidates are interviewed in the final phase, two will get a rejection. And while it feels disappointing, bear in mind that you have been up against candidates who were probably as qualified as you. So if you get a rejection after an interview, frame it constructively: it was a *success* that you made it *this far*.

Then, use the same framing when you respond to the rejection, because new similar job openings may be coming soon again from the same employer. If you show resilience and great character even when confronted by something as disappointing as a rejection, your chances of being considered again grow significantly.

Constructively framing the rejection in this manner, a good approach to answer it is:

- Thank those who interviewed you.

- Tell them you're still interested in a job in their organization should another opportunity arise.

- Ask for feedback. It may not be easy to get candid feedback, but try. For example, you may get valuable feedback about your interview skills or about some technical skills you could improve.

- Make your response customized by saying something positive that you sincerely mean about the process, the organization, the projects, the people, etc.

Step 24: Tie Up the Loose Ends

You have one last important task to do after you've signed your contract. Contact all the organizations where you have an open application and let them know you're no longer available, as you have accepted another offer. If you made it to the interview phase, thank them for their interest and express that you've enjoyed meeting them and provide some positive impressions about their organization. Also, consider adding them to your network (e.g., via LinkedIn); that is totally appropriate if you've had some good interactions during the process.

Finally, constructively participate in background checks, drug tests, or other formalities regarding your new job that your new organization may require.

ACKNOWLEDGMENTS

When deciding to start the long journey of writing this book, we knew that we needed a group of people with skills and experiences to complement our own to help shape the content and give honest feedback. Since many of the skills and behaviors in this book are difficult to define and thus require in-depth group discussions to get the messages right and define them into practical how-to advice, we asked ourselves, "Who's best at these skills and, at the same time, have high personal integrity and their hearts in the right place?" The choice fell on Kirsten Mathiasen, Dorte Prip, and Peter Mikkelsen, who all graciously agreed to help us. This team made this book much better than we could have done on our own by commenting and discussing our ideas and giving feedback on each chapter draft. And—as it should be—their comments were unfiltered and direct, including sometimes-blunt statements like, "That's boring" and "That's too long" and "That's repetitive." We recorded each and every of the more than twenty-five video discussions we had so we could harness all their good thoughts and wisdom. We are so grateful for their competent and loyal support.

Additionally, we owe big thanks to another group of experienced and capable individuals who generously read and commented on the final manuscript: Boel Enjin, Vera Lannek, Yu Cao, Claus Nissen, Fabio Nicolo, Hasse Groth, Lars Frahm, Michael Gerstlauer, and Thim Otskov. Their candid comments enhanced the final version of the book.

NOTES

In addition to our own experience and that of our expert panel, we have drawn inspiration from a number of great books. They are listed below and are recommended as supplemental reading for anyone interested in further exploration.

- Roger R. Pearman and Sarah C. Albritton, *I'm Not Crazy, I'm Just Not You* (Boston: Nicholas Brealey Publishing, 2020), Kindle Edition.

- Rosanne J. Thomas, *Excuse Me: The Survival Guide to Modern Business Etiquette* (New York: AMACOM, 2017), Kindle Edition.

- Peter F. Drucker, *The Effective Executive: The Definitive Guide to Getting the Right Things Done* (HarperCollins, 2017), Kindle Edition.

- David L. Blustein, *The Psychology of Working: A New Perspective for Career Development, Counseling, and Public Policy* (Mahwah, New Jersey: Lawrence Erlbaum Publishers, 2006), Kindle Edition.

- Jeffrey Pfeffer, *Power: Why Some People Have It—and Others Don't* (HarperCollins, 2010), Kindle Edition.

- Aaron T. Beck and Judith S. Beck, *Cognitive Behavior Therapy, Second Edition: Basics and Beyond* (New York: The Guilford Press, 2011), Kindle Edition.

- Albert Bandura, *Self-Efficacy: The Exercise of Control* (New York: W. H. Freeman, 2012).

- Seth J. Gillihan, *Cognitive Behavioral Therapy Made Simple: 10 Strategies for Managing Anxiety, Depression, Anger, Panic, and Worry* (Emeryville, California: Althea Press, 2018), Kindle Edition.

- Amy Cuddy, *Presence: Bringing Your Boldest Self to Your Biggest Challenges* (New York: Little, Brown Spark, 2018), Kindle Edition.

- Marshall Goldsmith, *What Got You Here Won't Get You There* (London: Profile Books, 2009), Kindle Edition.

- Patrick Lencioni, *The Five Dysfunctions of a Team: A Leadership Fable* (New York: Jossey-Bass, 2010), Kindle Edition.

- Marcus Buckingham and Ashley Goodall, *Nine Lies About Work: A Freethinking Leader's Guide to the Real World* (Boston, Massachusetts: Harvard Business Review Press, 2019), Kindle Edition.

- John C. Maxwell, *The 21 Irrefutable Laws of Leadership: Follow Them and People Will Follow You* (Nashville, Tennessee: Thomas Nelson, 2007), Kindle Edition.

- Christopher Peterson and Martin E. P. Seligman, *Character Strengths and Virtues: A Handbook and Classification* (Oxford: Oxford University Press, 2004), Kindle Edition.

- David D. Burns, *Feeling Good: The New Mood Therapy* (New York: HarperCollins, 2012), Kindle Edition.

- Clayton M. Christensen, James Allworth, and Karen Dillon, *How Will You Measure Your Life?* (New York: HarperCollins US, 2012), Kindle Edition.

- Susan Peppercorn, *Ditch Your Inner Critic at Work: Evidence-Based Strategies to Thrive in Your Career* (Dover, Massachusetts: Positive Workplace Partners, 2017), Kindle Edition.

- Brené Brown, *Rising Strong* (London: Ebury Publishing, 2015), Kindle Edition.

- Carl R. Rogers, *On Becoming a Person: A Therapist's View of Psychotherapy* (London: Constable & Robinson, 2011), Kindle Edition.

- Donald O. Clifton and Gallup Organization, *First, Break All the Rules: What the World's Greatest Managers Do Differently* (New York: Gallup Press, 2016).

- Douglas Stone and Sheila Heen, *Thanks for the Feedback: The Science and Art of Receiving Feedback Well* (UK: Portfolio Penguin, 2015), Kindle Edition.

- Heidi Grant Halvorson, *Succeed: How We Can Reach Our Goals* (New York: Plume, 2014), Kindle Edition.

- Mark L. Savickas, "Career Construction Theory and Practice," in *Career Development and Counseling: Putting Theory and Research to Work, Second Edition*, ed. Steven D. Brown and Robert W. Lent (Hoboken, New Jersey: Wiley, 2013).

- Stephen R Covey, *The 7 Habits of Highly Effective People* (New York: RosettaBooks, 2013), Kindle Edition.

- Martin E. P. Seligman, *Learned Optimism: How to Change Your Mind and Your Life* (New York: Knopf Doubleday Publishing Group, 2011), Kindle Edition.

- Charles Feltman, *The Thin Book of Trust: An Essential Primer for Building Trust at Work* (Bend, Oregon: Thin Book Publishing, 2009), Kindle Edition.

- Ira Chaleff, *The Courageous Follower: Standing Up to and for Our Leaders* (San Francisco, California: Berrett-Koehler Publishers, 2009), Kindle Edition.

- Kerry Patterson, Joseph Grenny, Ron McMillan, and Al Switzler, *Crucial Conversations: Tools for Talking When Stakes Are High, Second Edition* (New York: McGraw-Hill, 2012), Kindle Edition.

- Andrew Newberg and Mark Robert Waldman, *Words Can Change Your Brain: 12 Conversation Strategies to Build Trust, Resolve Conflict, and Increase Intimacy* (New York: Plume, 2014), Kindle Edition.

- Gabriel Weinberg and Lauren McCann, *Super Thinking: Upgrade Your Reasoning and Make Better Decisions with Mental Models* (London: Penguin, 2019), Kindle Edition.

- Irving L. Janis, *Groupthink: Psychological Studies of Policy Decisions and Fiascoes*, Second Edition (Boston: Houghton Mifflin Company, 1982).

- Robert B. Cialdini, *Influence: The Psychology of Persuasion* (New York: Harper Business, 2021), Kindle Edition.

- Katharine Brooks, *You Majored in What?: Designing Your Path from College to Career* (New York: Penguin Random House, 2017), Kindle Edition.

ABOUT THE AUTHORS

Peter Scheele is a writer with a long career in management, business, and IT. He's worked with global organizations like Siemens, Maersk, and Teradata and in diverse industries including retail, manufacturing, health care, finance, shipping, gaming, and government. When he's not absorbed in his work, he enjoys traveling, reading, cooking stews, and playing backgammon. He lives in Denmark.

Nina Bech-Andersen enjoyed a diverse international career for many years. From technical designs for the world's largest ship engines to negotiating multi-million-dollar contracts, Nina brought ingenuity and passion to every job. She is from North Yorkshire, UK, and has lived most of her adult life in Denmark. Nina enjoys running to stay fit and clear her head.

Printed in the USA
CPSIA information can be obtained
at www.ICGtesting.com
LVHW011114020124
767920LV00013B/649